48

50p

# HARRAP

# French
## phrasebook

Lola Busuttil

Valerie Grundy

# HARRAP

First published by Chambers Harrap Publishers Ltd 2006
7 Hopetoun Crescent
Edinburgh EH7 4AY

ISBN 0550 10281 7 (UK)
ISBN 978 0 245 50658 1 (France)

*Editor & Project Manager*
Anna Stevenson

*Publishing Manager*
Patrick White

*Prepress*
Susan Lawrie
Vienna Leigh

Réimprimé 2007, 2008

Designed and typeset by Chambers Harrap Publishers Ltd, Edinburgh
Printed and bound by Tien Wah Press (PTE.) LTD., Singapore
Illustrations by Art Explosion

# CONTENTS

# INTRODUCTION

This brand new English-French phrasebook from Harrap is ideal for anyone wishing to try out their foreign language skills while travelling abroad. The information is practical and clearly presented, helping you to overcome the language barrier and mix with the locals.

Each section features a list of useful words and a selection of common phrases: some of these you will read or hear, while others will help you to express yourself. The simple phonetic transcription system, specifically designed for English speakers, ensures that you will always make yourself understood.

The book also includes a mini bilingual dictionary of around 4,500 words, so that more adventurous users can build on the basic structures and engage in more complex conversations.

Concise information on local culture and customs is provided, along with practical tips to save you time. After all, you're on holiday – time to relax and enjoy yourself! There is also a food and drink glossary to help you make sense of menus, and ensure that you don't miss out on any of the national or regional specialities.

Remember that any effort you make will be appreciated. So don't be shy – have a go!

## ABBREVIATIONS USED IN THIS GUIDE

| | | | |
|---|---|---|---|
| *adj* | adjective | *n* | noun |
| *adv* | adverb | *pl* | plural |
| *f* | feminine | *prep* | preposition |
| *fpl* | feminine plural | *pron* | pronoun |
| *m* | masculine | *sing* | singular |
| *mf* | both masculine and feminine eg artiste *mf* | | |
| *m,f* | masculine form and feminine ending eg débutant(e) *m,f* | | |
| *mpl* | masculine plural | *v* | verb |

# PRONUNCIATION

Every phrase given in French in this guide is followed by its pronunciation, shown in italics. You just need to pronounce the phrase in the way shown in the simple phonetic transcription in order to make yourself understood by a French person. You don't need to worry about which part of a word to stress. Unlike English, French does not stress any particular syllable. And don't hesitate to ask a French person to show you how to pronounce any sounds you find difficult!

The main thing that makes French sound so different to English speakers is the use of nasalization. This refers to sounds that are produced more through the nose than the mouth. We have used the following two codes to show these:

*ON*    For the nasalized sounds **on**, **en**, **em**, **an** and **am** and a few other combinations in French. Try saying the English word "gong" and stopping short of pronouncing the full "ng" sound. Examples : **montre** *mONtr*, **entrée** *ON-tray*, **flan** *flON*, **ambassade** *ON-ba-sad*

*AN*    For the nasalized sounds **un** and **in** and a few other combinations in French. Try saying the English word "van" and stopping just short of pronouncing the "n". Examples: **quelqu'un** *kel-kAN*, **coussin** *koo-sAN*

The following code transcribes the French **u** sound:

*U*    To pronounce the "u" in French, try pursing your lips as if you were going to say "oo" and then, keeping them like that, trying to say "ee". Note that it is the written French **ou** that is pronounced simply as "oo". Examples: **bus** *bUs* – as opposed to – **route** *root*

Note also the following transcriptions:

*ey*    Used to show the pronunciation of **-eil** and **-eille**, rather as in English "survey" but slightly pronouncing the "ee" sound of the "y" at the end. Examples: **bouteille** *boo-tey*

*oy*    Used to show the pronunciation of the combination **-euil** rather as in English "boy" but slightly pronouncing the "ee" sound of the "y" at the end. Examples: **fauteuil** *fau-toy*

*uh*    Used to show the pronunciation of **e**, **eu** and some other combinations in certain words. Examples: **le** *luh*, **feu** *fuh*, **œuf** *uhf*.

| | | |
|---|---|---|
| **zh** | | Used to show the pronunciation of **j** and soft **g**. This is exactly the sound of the "s" in the English word "measure". Examples: **jaloux** *zha-loo*, **nager** *na-zhay* |

Some consonants are pronounced differently in French. Here is a guide to these along with their pronunciation:

| | | |
|---|---|---|
| **h** | not aspirated in French | Example: **habiter** *a-bee-tay* |
| **qu** | k | Example: **quai** *kay* |
| **r** | the "r" in French is vibrated at the back of your palate rather than against the teeth as in English | |
| **w** | v | Example: **wagon** *va-gON* |

Pronouncing accented vowels:

| | |
|---|---|
| **à**, **â** | *a* (as in English "cat") |
| **é** | *ay* (as in English "pay") |
| **è**, **ê** | *e* (as in English "pet") |

A few common French word endings and how to pronounce them:

| | |
|---|---|
| **-at** | *-ah* |
| **-eau** | *-oh* |
| **-et** | *-ay* |
| **-ez** | *-ay* |
| **-ot** | *-oh* |

Note also that the "**s**" plural ending is not usually pronounced in French: Example: **chats** *sha*

# Alphabet

How to pronounce the letters of the alphabet in French when you are spelling a word :

| | | | | | |
|---|---|---|---|---|---|
| **a** | *ah* | **j** | *zhee* | **s** | *ess* |
| **b** | *bay* | **k** | *ka* | **t** | *tay* |
| **c** | *say* | **l** | *el* | **u** | *U* |
| **d** | *day* | **m** | *em* | **v** | *vay* |
| **e** | *uh* | **n** | *en* | **w** | *doo-bluh-vay* |
| **f** | *ef* | **o** | *oh* | **x** | *eeks* |
| **g** | *zhay* | **p** | *pay* | **y** | *ee grek* |
| **h** | *ash* | **q** | *kU* | **z** | *zed* |
| **i** | *ee* | **r** | *er* | | |

# EVERYDAY CONVERSATION

In France, relations between people who do not know one another well tend to be fairly formal. There are two ways of saying "you" in French: the informal **tu** and the formal **vous**. **Tu** is used when speaking to one person you know well. **Vous** is used in formal or professional situations, and with people you don't know, such as sales assistants and waiting staff. If in doubt, you should always use the **vous** form, which is used to address one person or more than one. Note, however, that **vous** is also the plural form of **tu**, used when you are addressing more than one person you know well, for instance a group of friends.

When greeting people, **bonjour** (hello) is used during the day. **Bonsoir** (good evening) can be used from late afternoon onwards and may be used when arriving or leaving. **Bonne nuit** (goodnight) is only used before going to bed.

## The basics

| | |
|---|---|
| bye | au revoir *oh ruh-vwar*, (informal) salut *sa-lU* |
| excuse me | excusez-moi *eks-kUsay-mwa* |
| good afternoon | bonjour *bON-zhoor* |
| goodbye | au revoir *oh ruh-vwar* |
| good evening | bonsoir *bON-swar* |
| good morning | bonjour *bON-zhoor* |
| goodnight | bonne nuit *bon nwee* |
| hello | bonjour *bON-zhoor* |
| hi | bonjour *bON-zhoor*, (informal) salut *sa-lU* |
| no | non *nON* |
| OK | d'accord *da-kor*, (informal) ok *okay* |
| please | (informal) s'il te plaît *seel tuh play*, (polite or plural) s'il vous plaît *seel voo play* |

| thanks, thank you | merci *mer-see* |
| yes | oui *wee* |

## Expressing yourself

**I'd like ...**
je voudrais .../j'aimerais ...
*zhuh voo-dray .../zhay-muh-ray ...*

**we'd like ...**
nous voudrions .../nous aimerions ...
*noo voo-dree-yON .../nooz ay-muh-ree-yON ...*

**do you want ...?**
est-ce que vous voulez ... ?
*ess-kuh voo voo-lay ... ?*

**do you have ...?**
est-ce que vous auriez ... ?
*ess-kuh vooz ohr-yay ... ?*

**is there a ...?**
est-ce qu'il y a un/une ... ?
*ess-keel ya AN/Un ... ?*

**are there any ...?**
est-ce qu'il y a des ... ?
*ess-keel ya day ... ?*

**how ...?**
comment ... ?
*koh-mON ... ?*

**why ...?**
pourquoi ... ?
*poor-kwa ... ?*

**when ...?**
quand ... ?
*kON ... ?*

**what ...?**
qu'est-ce que ... ?
*kess-kuh ... ?*

**where is ...?**
où est ... ?
*oo ay ... ?*

**where are ...?**
où sont ... ?
*oo sON ... ?*

**how much is it?**
c'est combien ?
*say kON-byAN ?*

**what is it?**
qu'est-ce que c'est ?
*kess-kuh say ?*

**do you speak English?**
est-ce que vous parlez anglais ?
*ess-kuh voo par-lay ON-glay ?*

**where are the toilets, please?**
s'il vous plaît, où sont les toilettes ?
*seel voo play, oo sON lay twa-let ?*

**how are you?** *(informal)*
comment vas-tu ?
*koh-mON va-tU ?*

**how are you?** *(polite or plural)*
comment allez-vous ?
*koh-mONt a-lay-voo ?*

**fine, thanks**
bien, merci
*byAN, mer-see*

**thanks very much**
merci beaucoup
*mer-see boh-koo*

**no, thanks**
non merci
*nON mer-see*

**yes, please**
oui, merci
*wee, mer-see*

**you're welcome**
il n'y a pas de quoi
*eel nya pa duh kwa*

**see you later**
à tout à l'heure
*a toot a luhr*

**I'm sorry**
je suis désolé
*zhuh swee day-zoh-lay*

## Understanding

| | |
|---|---|
| **attention** | warning |
| **entrée** | entrance |
| **gratuit** | free |
| **hors service** | out of order |
| **interdiction de ...** | do not ... |
| **ouvert** | open |
| **réservé** | reserved |
| **sortie** | exit |
| **stationnement interdit** | no parking |
| **toilettes** | toilets |

**il y a ...**
there's/there are ...

**bienvenue**
welcome

**est-ce que ça vous dérange si ... ?**
do you mind if ...?

**un instant, s'il vous plaît**
one moment, please

**asseyez-vous, je vous en prie**
please take a seat

# PROBLEMS UNDERSTANDING FRENCH

## Expressing yourself

**pardon?**
pardon ?
*par-dON ?*

**what?**
quoi ?
*kwa ?*

**could you repeat that, please?**
vous pouvez répéter ?
*voo poo-vay ray-pay-tay ?*

**could you speak more slowly?**
est-ce que vous pourriez parler plus lentement ?
*ess-kuh voo poor-yay par-lay plU lON-tuh-mON ?*

**I don't understand**
je ne comprends pas
*zhuh nuh kON-prON pa*

**I understand a little French**
je comprends un peu le français
*zhuh kON-prON AN puh luh frON-say*

**I can understand French but I can't speak it**
je comprends le français mais je ne le parle pas
*zhuh kON-prON luh frON-say may zhuh nuh luh parl pa*

**I hardly speak any French**
je parle à peine français
*zhuh parl a pen frON-say*

**do you speak English?**
est-ce que vous parlez anglais ?
*ess-kuh voo par-lay ON-glay ?*

**how do you say … in French?**
comment dit-on … en français ?
*koh-mON deet ON … ON frON-say ?*

**how do you spell it?**
comment ça s'écrit ?
*koh-mON sa say-kree ?*

**what's that called in French?**
comment ça s'appelle en français ?
*koh-mON sa sa-pel ON frON-say ?*

**could you write it down for me?**
est-ce que vous pourriez me l'écrire ?
*ess-kuh voo poor-yay muh lay-kreer ?*

### Understanding

**est-ce que vous comprenez le français ?**
do you understand French?

**je vais vous l'écrire**
I'll write it down for you

**ça veut dire …**
it means …

**c'est une sorte de …**
it's a kind of …

# SPEAKING ABOUT THE LANGUAGE

### Expressing yourself

**I learned a few words from my phrasebook**
j'ai appris quelques mots dans un guide de conversation
*zhay a-pree kel-kuh moh dONz AN geed duh kON-ver-sas-yON*

**I did it at school but I've forgotten everything**
j'en ai fait à l'école mais j'ai tout oublié
*zhON ay fayt a lay-kol may zhay toot oo-blee-yay*

**I can just about get by**
je me débrouille à peu près
*zhuh muh day-broo-ee a puh pray*

**I hardly know two words**
je connais à peine quelques mots
*zhu koh-nay a pen kel-kuh moh*

**I find French a difficult language**
je trouve que le français est une langue difficile
*zhuh troov kuh luh frON-say ayt Un lONg dee-fee-seel*

**I know the basics but no more than that**
je connais les bases mais pas plus
*zuh koh-nay lay baz may pa plUs*

**people speak too quickly for me**
les gens parlent trop vite
*lay zhON parl troh veet*

### Understanding

**vous avez un bon accent**
you have a good accent

**vous parlez très bien le français**
you speak very good French

# ASKING THE WAY

### Expressing yourself

**excuse me, can you tell me where … is, please?**
excusez-moi, pourriez-vous me dire où est … ?
*ek-skU-zay-mwa, poor-yay-voo muh deer oo ay … ?*

**which way is it to …?**
…, c'est par où ?
*…, say par oo ?*

**can you tell me how to get to …?**
pourriez-vous m'indiquer comment aller à … ?
*poor-yay-voo mAN-dee-kay koh-mON alay a … ?*

**is there a … near here?**
y a-t-il un/une … près d'ici ?
*ya-teel AN/Un … pray dee-see ?*

**could you show me on the map?**
pourriez-vous me montrer sur la carte ?
*poor-yay voo muh mON-tray sUr la kart ?*

**is there a map of the town somewhere?**
y a-t-il un plan de la ville quelque part ?
*ya-teel AN plON duh la veel kel-kuh par ?*

**is it far?**
c'est loin ?
*say lwAN ?*

**I'm looking for …**
je cherche …
*zhuh shersh …*

**I'm lost**
je suis perdu
*zhuh swee per-dU*

## Understanding

**allez/continuez tout droit**
go/carry on straight ahead

**tournez à gauche/à droite**
turn left/right

**descendez/montez jusqu'à ...**
go up/down until you get to ...

**vous êtes à pied ?**
are you on foot?

**c'est à cinq minutes en voiture**
it's five minutes away by car

**c'est la première/deuxième/troisième à gauche**
it's the first/second/third on the left

**tournez à droite au rond-point**
turn right at the roundabout

**tournez à gauche quand vous arrivez à la banque**
turn left at the bank

**prenez la prochaine sortie**
take the next exit

**ce n'est pas loin**
it's not far

**c'est à deux pas d'ici**
it's just round the corner

# GETTING TO KNOW PEOPLE

When meeting up with or being introduced to somebody in France, there is always a form of greeting. With people you don't know or between men, the custom is to shake hands. People who know each other well kiss each other on the cheek (**faire la bise**) when they meet. The number of kisses varies between two and four, according to the region.

## The basics

| | |
|---|---|
| **bad** | mauvais *moh-vay* |
| **beautiful** | beau *boh* |
| **boring** | ennuyeux *ON-nwee-yuh* |
| **cheap** | pas cher *pa sher* |
| **expensive** | cher *sher* |
| **good** | bon *bON* |
| **great** | génial *zhay-nyal* |
| **interesting** | intéressant *AN-tay-re-sON* |
| **nice** | *(good)* **bon** *bON*, *(pretty)* **joli** *zhoh-lee*, *(kind)* gentil *zhON-tee* |
| **not bad** | pas mal *pa mal* |
| **well** | bien *byAN* |
| **to hate** | détester *day-tes-tay* |
| **to like** | bien aimer *byANn ay-may* |
| **to love** | adorer *ah-doh-ray* |

# INTRODUCING YOURSELF AND FINDING OUT ABOUT OTHER PEOPLE

## Expressing yourself

**my name's ...**
je m'appelle ...
*zhuh ma-pel ...*

**how do you do!**
bonjour
*bON-zhoor*

**this is my husband**
je vous présente mon mari
*zhuh voo pray-zONt mON ma-ree*

**I'm English**
je suis anglais(e)
*zhuh sweez ON-glay(z)*

**I'm from ...**
je viens de ...
*zhuh vyAN duh ...*

**how old are you?**
quel âge as-tu ?
*kel azh a tU ?*

**what do you do for a living?**
qu'est-ce vous faites dans la vie ?
*kess-kuh voo fet dON la vee ?*

**I work**
je travaille
*zhuh tra-va-y*

**I'm a teacher**
je suis prof
*zhuh swee prof*

**what's your name?**
comment vous vous appelez ?
*koh-mON voo vooz a-play ?*

**pleased to meet you!**
enchanté !
*ON-shON-tay !*

**this is my partner, Karen**
je vous présente Karen, ma copine
*zhuh voo pray-zONt Karen, ma koh-peen*

**we're Welsh**
nous sommes gallois
*noo som gal-wa*

**where are you from?**
vous êtes d'où ?
*vooz et doo ?*

**I'm 22**
j'ai 22 ans
*zhay vANt-duhz ON*

**are you a student?**
tu es étudiant ?
*tU ay ay-tU-dyON ?*

**I'm studying law**
je fais des études de droit
*zhuh fay dayz ay-tUd duh drwa*

**I stay at home with the children**
je ne travaille pas, je m'occupe des enfants
*zhu nuh tra-va-y pa, zhuh mo-kUp dayz ON-fON*

**I work part-time**
je travaille à temps partiel
*zhuh tra-va-y a tON pars-yel*

**I work in marketing**
je travaille dans le marketing
*zhuh tra-va-y dON luh mar-ke-teeng*

**I'm retired**
je suis à la retraite
*zhuh sweez a la ruh-tret*

**I'm self-employed**
je travaille à mon compte
*zhuh tra-va-y a mON kONt*

**I have two children**
j'ai deux enfants
*zhay duhz ON-fON*

**we don't have any children**
nous n'avons pas d'enfants
*noo navON pa dON-fON*

**two boys and a girl**
deux garçons et une fille
*duh gar-sON ay Un fee*

**a boy of five and a girl of two**
un garçon de cinq ans et une fille de deux ans
*AN gar-sON duh sANk ON ay Un fee duh duhz ON*

**have you ever been to Britain?**
est-ce que vous êtes déjà allé en Grande-Bretagne ?
*ess-kuh vooz et day-zha alay ON grONd-bruh-tan-yuh ?*

## Understanding

**vous êtes anglais ?**
are you English?

**je connais assez bien l'Angleterre**
I know England quite well

**nous aussi, on est en vacances ici**
we're on holiday here too

**j'aimerais beaucoup aller en Écosse un jour**
I'd love to go to Scotland one day

# TALKING ABOUT YOUR STAY

## Expressing yourself

**we're on holiday**
nous sommes en vacances
*noo somz ON va-kONs*

**I'm here on business**
je suis ici pour mon travail
*zhuh sweez ee-see poor mON tra-va-y*

**we've been here for a week**
ça fait une semaine qu'on est ici
*sa fay Un suh-men kON ayt ee-see*

**I arrived three days ago**
je suis arrivé il y a trois jours
*zhuh sweez a-ree-vay eel ya trwa zhoor*

**I'm only here for a long weekend**
je ne suis ici que pour un long week-end
*zhuh nuh sweez ee-see kuh poor AN lON wee-kend*

**we're just passing through**
on est seulement de passage
*ON ay suhl-mON duh pa-sazh*

**we're on our honeymoon**
c'est notre voyage de noces
*say not-ruh vwa-yazh duh nos*

**this is our first time in France**
c'est la première fois que nous venons en France
*say la pruhm-yer fwa kuh noo vuh-nON ON frONs*

**we're here to celebrate our wedding anniversary**
nous sommes ici pour notre anniversaire de mariage
*noo somz ee-see poor notr a-nee-ver-ser duh mar-yazh*

**we're here with friends**
on est ici avec des amis
*ON ayt ee-see avek dayz amee*

**we're touring around**
on visite la région
*ON vee-zeet la rayzh-yON*

**we managed to get a cheap flight**
on a trouvé un vol pas cher
*ON a troo-vay AN vol pa sher*

**we're thinking about buying a house here**
nous pensons à acheter une maison ici
*noo pON-sONz a ash-tay Un may-zON ee-see*

## Understanding

**bonnes vacances !**
have a good holiday!

**bon séjour !**
enjoy your stay!

**bonne fin de vacances !**
enjoy the rest of your holiday!

**à la prochaine !**
see you!

**c'est la première fois que vous venez dans la vallée de la Loire ?**
is this your first time in the Loire Valley?

**vous êtes ici pour combien de temps ?**
how long are you staying?

**ça te/vous plaît (ici) ?**
do you like it here?

**est-ce que vous avez été à … ?**
have you been to …?

## STAYING IN TOUCH

### Expressing yourself

**we should stay in touch**
on reste en contact, hein ?
*ON rest ON kON-takt, AN ?*

**I'll give you my e-mail address**
je vais vous donner mon adresse e-mail
*zhuh vay voo doh-nay mONn a-dres ee-mayl*

**here's my address, if ever you come to Britain**
voilà mon adresse, si vous venez un jour en Grande-Bretagne
*wwa-la mONn a-dres, see voo vuh-nay AN zhoor ON grONd-bruh-tan-yuh*

### Understanding

**tu me donnes ton adresse ?**
will you give me your address?

**est-ce que vous avez une adresse e-mail ?**
do you have an e-mail address?

**vous êtes toujours les bienvenus chez nous**
you're always welcome to come and stay with us here

# EXPRESSING YOUR OPINION

> **Some informal expressions**
> **c'était nul** it was a complete waste of time
> **c'était chiant** it was deadly boring
> **on s'est bien éclatés** we had a fantastic time

## Expressing yourself

**I really like …**
j'aime beaucoup …
*zhem boh-koo …*

**I really liked …**
j'ai vraiment aimé …
*zhay vray-mON ay-may …*

**I don't like …**
je n'aime pas …
*zhuh nem pa …*

**I didn't like …**
je n'ai pas aimé …
*zhuh nay paz ay-may …*

**I love …**
j'adore …
*zha-dor …*

**I loved …**
j'ai adoré …
*zhay a-doh-ray …*

**I would like …**
j'aimerais …
*zhe-muh-ray …*

**I would have liked …**
j'aurais aimé …
*zhoh-ray ay-may …*

**I find it …**
je trouve ça …
*zhuh troov sa …*

**I found it …**
j'ai trouvé ça …
*zhay troo-vay sa …*

**it's lovely**
c'est magnifique
*say ma-nee-feek*

**it was lovely**
c'était magnifique
*say-tay ma-nee-feek*

**I agree**
je suis d'accord
*zhuh swee da-kor*

**I don't agree**
je ne suis pas d'accord
*zhuh nuh swee pa da-kor*

**I don't know**
je ne sais pas
*zhuh nuh say pa*

**I don't mind**
ça m'est égal
*sa met ay-gal*

GETTING TO
KNOW PEOPLE

19

**GETTING TO KNOW PEOPLE**

**I don't like the sound of it**
ça ne me dit rien
*sa nuh muh dee ree-AN*

**it sounds interesting**
ça a l'air intéressant
*sa a ler AN-tay-re-sON*

**it really annoys me**
ça m'énerve vraiment
*sa may-nerv vray-mON*

**it was boring**
c'était ennuyeux
*say-tay ON-nwee-yuh*

**it's a rip-off**
c'est de l'arnaque
*say duh lar-nak*

**it gets very busy at night**
c'est très animé le soir
*say trayz a-nee-may luh swar*

**it's too busy**
il y a trop de monde
*eel ya troh duh mONd*

**it's very quiet**
il n'y a pas grand monde
*eel nya pa grON mONd*

**I really enjoyed myself**
je me suis bien amusé
*zhuh muh swee byAN a-mU-zay*

**we had a great time**
c'était super
*say-tay sU-per*

**there was a really good atmosphere**
il y avait une ambiance très sympa
*eel ya-vay Un ON-byONs tray sAN-pa*

**we found a great hotel**
on a trouvé un hôtel très bien
*ON a troo-vay AN oh-tel tray byAN*

**we met some nice people**
on a rencontré des gens sympas
*ON a rON-kON-tray day zhON sAN-pa*

## Understanding

**est-ce que tu aimes/vous aimez … ?**
do you like …?

**vous avez passé du bon temps ?**
did you enjoy yourselves?

**je vous recommande …**
I recommend …

**vous devriez aller à …**
you should go to …

**c'est une très belle région**
it's a lovely area

**ce n'est pas trop touristique**
there aren't too many tourists

**n'y allez pas le week-end, il y a trop de monde**
don't go at the weekend, it's too busy

# TALKING ABOUT THE WEATHER

> **Some informal expressions**
>
> **il faisait un froid de canard** it was freezing cold
> **il faisait une chaleur à crever** it was scorching
> **il tombait des cordes** it was pouring with rain

## Expressing yourself

**have you seen the weather forecast for tomorrow?**
est-ce que vous avez vu la météo pour demain ?
*ess-kuh vooz avay vU la may-tay-oh poor duh-mAN ?*

**it's going to be nice**
il va faire beau
*eel va fer boh*

**it isn't going to be nice**
il ne va pas faire beau
*eel nuh va pa fer boh*

**it's really hot**
il fait vraiment chaud
*eel fay vray-mON shoh*

**it gets cold at night**
il fait froid la nuit
*eel fay frwa la nwee*

**the weather was beautiful**
il a fait un temps superbe
*eel a fay AN tON sU-perb*

**it rained a few times**
il a plu quelques fois
*eel a plU kel-kuh fwa*

**there was a thunderstorm**
il y a eu un orage
*eel ya U AN oh-razh*

**it's been lovely all week**
il a fait beau toute la semaine
*eel a fay boh toot la suh-men*

**we've been lucky with the weather**
on a eu de la chance avec le temps
*ON a U duh la shONs avek luh tON*

## Understanding

**il paraît qu'il va pleuvoir**
it's supposed to rain

**il va encore faire chaud demain**
it's going to be hot again tomorrow

**ils ont prévu du beau temps pour le reste de la semaine**
they've forecast good weather for the rest of the week

21

## The basics

| | |
|---|---|
| airport | aéroport *ah-ay-roh-por* |
| boarding | embarquement *ON-bar-kuh-mON* |
| boarding card | carte d'embarquement *kart dON-bar-kuh-mON* |
| boat | bateau *ba-toh* |
| bus | bus *bUs* |
| bus station | gare routière *gar roo-tyer* |
| bus stop | arrêt de bus *a-ray duh bUs* |
| car | voiture *vwa-tUr* |
| check-in | enregistrement *ON-ruh-zhees-truh-mON* |
| coach | autocar *oh-toh-kar*, car *kar* |
| coach station | gare routière *gar roo-tyer* |
| ferry | ferry *fay-ree* |
| flight | vol *vol* |
| gate | porte (d'embarquement) *port (dON-bar-kuh-mON)* |
| left-luggage (office) | (bureau des) objets trouvés *(bU-roh dayz) ob-zhay troo-vay* |
| luggage | bagages *ba-gazh* |
| map | carte *kart* |
| motorway | autoroute *oh-toh-root* |
| passport | passeport *pas-por* |
| plane | avion *av-yON* |
| platform | quai *kay* |
| railway station | gare *gar* |
| return (ticket) | aller-retour *alay-ruh-toor* |
| road | route *root*; (street) rue *rU* |
| shuttle bus | navette *na-vet* |
| single (ticket) | aller (simple) *alay (sANpl)* |
| street | rue *rU* |
| streetmap | plan (de la ville) *plAN (duh la veel)* |
| taxi | taxi *tak-see* |
| terminal | terminal *ter-mee-nal* |
| ticket | (for bus, underground) ticket *tee-kay*, (for train, plane) billet *bee-yay* |

| | |
|---|---|
| **timetable** | horaires *o-rer* |
| **town centre** | centre-ville *sON-truh-veel* |
| **train** | train *trAN* |
| **tram** | tramway *tramway* |
| **underground** | métro *may-troh* |
| **underground station** | station de métro *stass-yON duh may-troh* |
| **to book** | réserver *ray-zer-vay* |
| **to hire** | louer *loo-ay* |

### Expressing yourself

**where can I buy tickets?**
où est-ce que je peux acheter des billets ?
*oo ess-kuh zhuh puh ash-tay day bee-yay ?*

**a ticket to ..., please**
un billet pour ...
*AN bee-yay poor ...*

**I'd like to book a ticket**
je voudrais réserver un billet
*zhuh voo-dray ray-zer-vay AN bee-yay*

**how much is a ticket to ...?**
combien coûte un billet pour ... ?
*kom-byAN koot AN bee-yay poor ... ?*

**are there any concessions for students?**
est-ce qu'il y a des réductions pour les étudiants ?
*ess keel ya day ray-dUk-syON poor layz ay-tU-dyAN ?*

**could I have a timetable, please?**
est-ce que je peux avoir un dépliant avec les horaires ?
*ess kuh zhuh puh av-war AN day-plee-yAN avek layz o-rer ?*

**is there an earlier/later one?**
y en a-t-il un plus tôt/tard ?
*yON-a-teel AN plU toh/tar ?*

**how long does the journey take?**
combien de temps dure le voyage ?
*kom-byAN duh tON dUr luh vwa-yazh ?*

**is this seat free?**
est-ce que cette place est libre ?
*ess kuh set plass ay leebr ?*

**I'm sorry, there's someone sitting there**
désolé, il y a déjà quelqu'un
*day-zoh-lay, eel ya day-zha kel-kAN*

## Understanding

### Making sense of abbreviations

**A/R** (= aller-retour) return (ticket)
**Arr** (= arrivée) arrival
**Dép** (= départ) departure
**PC** (= petite ceinture) Paris inner ring road
**RER** (= réseau express régional) express train network in the Paris region
**SNCF** (= Société nationale des chemins de fer français) French national rail company
**TER** (= train express régional) regional express train
**TGV** (= train à grande vitesse) high speed train

Days of the week: **lun**, **mar**, **mer**, **jeu**, **ven**, **sam**, **dim**, or **lu**, **ma**, **me**, **je**, **ve**, **sa**, **di**.
On timetables, **tlj** stands for **tous les jours** (every day), and **sf dim** for **sauf le dimanche** (except Sundays).

| | |
|---|---|
| **accueil** | information |
| **annulé** | cancelled |
| **arrivées** | arrivals |
| **billeterie** | tickets |
| **billeterie automatique** | ticket machine |
| **correspondances** | connections |
| **départs** | departures |
| **entrée** | entrance |
| **renseignements** | information |
| **retardé** | delayed |
| **sortie** | exit |
| **toilettes** | toilets |

**il ne reste plus de places**
there are no seats left

**tout est complet**
everything is fully booked

# BY PLANE

## Expressing yourself

**where's the British Airways check-in?**
où est l'enregistrement des bagages pour British Airways ?
*oo ay lON-ruh-zhees-truh-mON day ba-gazh poor British Airways ?*

**I've got an e-ticket**
j'ai acheté mon billet sur Internet
*zhay ash-tay mON bee-yay sUr AN-ter-net*

**one suitcase and one piece of hand luggage**
une valise et un bagage à main
*Un va-leez ay AN ba-gazh a mAN*

**what time do we board?**
à quelle heure embarque-t-on ?
*a kel uhr ON-bar-kuh-tON ?*

**I'd like to confirm my return flight**
je voudrais confirmer mon vol de retour
*zhuh voo-dray kON-feer-may mON vol duh ruh-toor*

**one of my suitcases is missing**
il me manque une valise
*eel muh mONk Un va-leez*

**my luggage hasn't arrived**
mes bagages ne sont pas arrivés
*may ba-gazh nuh sON paz a-ree-vay*

**I've missed my connection**
j'ai raté ma correspondance
*zhay ra-tay ma ko-res-pON-dONs*

**the plane was two hours late**
l'avion a eu deux heures de retard
*lav-yON a U duhz uhr duh ruh-tar*

**I've left something on the plane**
j'ai oublié quelque chose dans l'avion
*zhay oo-blee-yay kel-kuh-shohz dAN lav-yON*

**I want to report the loss of my luggage**
je voudrais faire une déclaration de perte pour mes bagages
*zhuh voo-dray fer Un day-kla-ra-syON duh pert poor may ba-gazh*

## Understanding

| | |
|---|---|
| **contrôle des passeports** | passport control |
| **douane** | customs |

| **embarquement immédiat** | immediate boarding |
| **enregistrement** | check-in |
| **marchandises à déclarer** | goods to declare |
| **ressortissants de l'UE** | EU passport holders |
| **retrait des bagages** | baggage reclaim |
| **rien à déclarer** | nothing to declare |
| **salle d'embarquement** | departure lounge |
| **vols intérieurs** | domestic flights |

**veuillez patienter dans la salle d'embarquement**
please wait in the departure lounge

**voulez-vous une place côté hublot ou côté couloir ?**
would you like a window seat or an aisle seat?

**vous avez une correspondance à …**
you'll have to change in …

**combien de bagages avez-vous ?**
how many bags do you have?

**avez-vous fait vous-même tous vos bagages ?**
did you pack all your bags yourself?

**quelqu'un vous a-t-il donné quelque chose à emporter à bord ?**
has anyone given you anything to take on board?

**vous avez un excédent de cinq kilos**
your luggage is five kilos overweight

**voilà votre carte d'embarquement**
here's your boarding card

**l'embarquement commencera à …**
boarding will begin at …

**veuillez vous rendre à la porte numéro …**
please proceed to gate number …

**dernier appel pour …**
this is a final call for …

**vous pouvez appeler ce numéro pour savoir si vos bagages sont
arrivés**
you can call this number to check that your luggage has arrived

# BY TRAIN, COACH, BUS, UNDERGROUND, TRAM

Tickets for all forms of public transport except buses need to be bought in advance. For high-speed trains (**TGV**) the ticket includes a seat reservation. The number of the coach (**voiture**) and the seat number (**place assise**) are marked on the ticket. For all trains you need to punch your ticket in one of the orange machines before going onto the platform. You should always note the number of the train. This is printed on the ticket eg TGV 9833. This is important since when you look at the indicator board in the station, it will only give the final destination of the train and not the stations it will stop at en route.

When you get on a bus or tram, there is a machine for you to punch your ticket. It is an offence not to do so.

When using the underground, you need to identify the end of the line for the line and direction you are going in. Indications such as northbound/southbound are not used.

## Expressing yourself

**can I have a map of the underground, please?**
est-ce que je pourrais avoir un plan du métro ?
*ess kuh zhuh poo-ray av-war AN plON dU may-troh ?*

**what time is the next train to ...?**
à quelle heure est le prochain train pour ... ?
*a kel uhr ay luh pro-shAN trAN poor ... ?*

**what time is the last train?**
à quelle heure part le dernier train ?
*a kel uhr par luh der-nyay trAN ?*

**which platform is it for the ... train?**
de quel quai part le train pour ... ?
*duh kel kay par luh trAN poor ... ?*

**where can I catch a bus to …?**
où est-ce que je peux prendre un bus pour … ?
*oo ess kuh juh puh prONdr AN bUs poor … ?*

**is this the stop for …?**
c'est bien l'arrêt pour … ?
*say byAN la-ray poor … ?*

**which line do I take to get to …?**
quelle ligne dois-je prendre pour … ?
*kel leen-yuh dwazh prONdr poor … ?*

**is this where the coach leaves for …?**
c'est bien d'ici que part le car pour … ?
*say byAN dee-see kuh par luh kar poor … ?*

**can you tell me when I need to get off?**
pourriez-vous me dire quand je dois descendre ?
*poor-yay voo muh deer kON zhuh dwa day-sONdr ?*

## Understanding

| | |
|---|---|
| **accès aux quais** | to the trains |
| **banlieue** | to suburban trains |
| **carte orange** | travel pass |
| **départs dans la journée** | tickets for travel today |
| **grandes lignes** | to main-line trains |
| **hebdomadaire** | weekly |
| **mensuel** | monthly |
| **réservations** | bookings |

**côté fenêtre ou côté couloir ?**
a window seat or an aisle seat?

**vous avez un changement à …**
you'll have to change at …

**il y a un arrêt un peu plus loin à droite**
there's a stop a bit further along on the right

**vous devez prendre le bus numéro …**
you need to get the number … bus

**allez jusqu'au terminus**
go to the terminus

**ce train dessert les gares de …**
this train calls at …

**le train en provenance de …**
the train arriving from …

**le train à destination de …**
the train for …

**le prochain arrêt est …**
the next stop is …

# BY CAR

France has an excellent road network with many toll motorways (**autoroutes**, signposted in blue and numbered A6, A7 etc) and dual carriageways (**routes à quatres voies**, signposted in red). The trunk roads (**routes nationales**), signposted in green and numbered ((R)N6, (R)N7 etc) are also good. It is always possible to take one of these instead of a toll motorway and many offer more scenic routes. Speed limits are 130 km/h on motorways and 120 km/h on dual carriageways. Unless otherwise stated, the speed limit in towns and villages is 50 km/h. There are regular stopping places (**aires**) on motorways. Signs indicate the facilities offered. At tollgates (**péages**) you can pay by card using an automatic machine at gates indicated **CB** (**carte bancaire**) and by card or cash at the staffed gates indicated with a green arrow. Note that French law obliges drivers to carry photo identity, driving licence, car registration papers and insurance details at all times. As in Britain, seatbelts are obligatory in both front and rear seats and the legal alcohol limit is just a little over half of what it is in Britain.

Taxi drivers will usually ask you to pay extra for luggage. Tipping is discretionary.

## Expressing yourself

**where can I find a petrol station?**
où est-ce que je peux trouver une station-service ?
*oo ess kuh zhuh puh troo-vay Un stass-yON ser-vees ?*

**lead-free petrol, please**
du sans-plomb, s'il vous plaît
*dU sON plON, seel voo play*

**how much is it per litre?**
c'est combien le litre ?
*say kON-byAN luh leetr ?*

**we got stuck in a traffic jam**
on a été bloqués dans un embouteillage
*ON na ay-tay blo-kay dONz AN ON-boo-tay-yazh*

**is there a garage near here?**
y a-t-il un garagiste par ici ?
*ya-teel AN ga-ra-zheest par ee-see ?*

**can you help us to push the car?**
pourriez-vous nous aider à pousser la voiture ?
*poor-yay voo nooz ay-day a poo-say la vwa-tUr ?*

**the battery's dead**
la batterie est morte
*la ba-tree ay mort*

**I've broken down**
je suis tombé en panne
*zhuh swee tON-bay ON pan*

**we've run out of petrol**
on est en panne d'essence
*ON nayt ON pan day-sONs*

**I've lost my car keys**
j'ai perdu mes clés de voiture
*zhay per-dU may klay duh vwa-tUr*

**I've got a puncture and my spare tyre is flat**
j'ai crevé et la roue de secours est à plat
*zhay kruh-vay ay la roo duh suh-koor ayt a pla*

**we've just had an accident**
nous venons d'avoir un accident
*noo vuh-nON da-vwar AN ak-si-dON*

**how long will it take to repair?**
ça va prendre combien de temps à réparer ?
*sa va prONdr kON-byAN duh tON a ray-pa-ray ?*

### ◆ Hiring a car

**I'd like to hire a car for a week**
je voudrais louer une voiture pour une semaine
*zhuh voo-dray loo-ay Un vwa-tUr poor Un suh-men*

**an automatic (car)**
une voiture à boîte de vitesses automatique
*Un vwa-tUr a bwat duh vee-tess oh-toh-ma-teek*

**we need a child seat**
nous aurions besoin d'un siège-auto pour enfant
*nooz oh-ryON buh-zwAN dAN syezh poor ON-fON*

## ◆ Getting a taxi

**is there a taxi rank near here?**
y a-t-il une station de taxis près d'ici ?
*ya-teel Un stass-yON duh tak-see pray dee-see ?*

**I'd like to go to …**
je vais à …
*zhuh vayz a …*

**I'd like to book a taxi for 8pm**
je voudrais un taxi pour 20 heures
*juh voo-dray AN tak-see poor vANt uhr*

**you can drop me off here, thanks**
vous pouvez m'arrêter ici, merci
*voo poo-vay ma-ray-tay ee-see, mer-see*

**how much will it be to go to the airport?**
combien ça va me coûter pour aller à l'aéroport ?
*kON-byAN sa va muh koo-tay poor alay a la-ay-roh-por ?*

## ◆ Hitchhiking

**I'm going to …**
je vais à …
*zhuh vayz a …*

**thanks for the lift**
merci de m'avoir emmené
*mer-see duh mav-war ON-mnay*

**can you drop me off here?**
est-ce que vous pourriez m'arrêter ici ?
*ess-kuh voo poor-yay ma-ray-tay ee-see ?*

**could you take me as far as …?**
pourriez-vous m'emmener jusqu'à … ?
*poor-yay voo mON-mnay zhUska … ?*

**we hitched a lift**
on a fait du stop
*ON na fay dU stop*

## Understanding

| | |
|---|---|
| **autres directions** | other directions |
| **bouchon** | congestion ahead |
| **complet** | full *(car park)* |
| **conservez votre ticket** | keep your ticket with you |

TRAVELLING

31

| | |
|---|---|
| **location de voitures** | car hire |
| **parking** | car park |
| **péage** | tollgate |
| **périphérique, périph** | ring road |
| **places libres** | spaces *(car park)* |
| **ralentissez** | slow down |
| **stationnement interdit** | no parking |
| **toutes directions** | all directions |

**il me faut votre permis de conduire, une pièce d'identité, un justificatif de domicile et votre carte de paiement**
I'll need your driving licence, another form of ID, proof of address and your credit card

**il y a une caution de 150 euros**
there's a 150 euro deposit

**c'est bon, montez, je vais vous avancer jusqu'à …**
OK, get in, I'll take you as far as …

# BY BOAT

## Expressing yourself

| | |
|---|---|
| **how long is the crossing?** | **I'm seasick** |
| combien dure la traversée ? | j'ai le mal de mer |
| *kON-byAN dUr la tra-ver-say ?* | *jay luh mal duh mer* |

## Understanding

| | |
|---|---|
| **passagers sans véhicule** | foot passengers only |
| **prochain départ à …** | next crossing at … |
| **traversée toutes les heures** | hourly crossings |

Hotels (**hôtels**) in France are classified according to a star system, as in the UK – and priced accordingly. Those classified by Logis de France generally offer a good standard of accommodation and food at a reasonable price. They publish a guide annually. Prices are usually displayed outside hotels. You can also find **chambres d'hôtes** (bed and breakfast). Some of these offer a **table d'hôte** service, providing lunch and/or dinner.

If you are looking for self-catering accommodation, the organization Gîtes de France offers a wide variety from **résidences de tourisme** (luxury service apartments) to **camping à la ferme** (camping on a farm). In between, there are **gîtes ruraux** (country cottages) and **chalets-loisirs** (small chalets in rural areas). The classification system for **gîtes** uses an ear of corn symbol (**épis**). All accommodation registered with Gîtes de France has to conform to certain standards. A comprehensive guide to Gîtes de France is available at bookstores in both France and the UK. They also have a website.

There are good youth hostels (**auberges de jeunesse**, abbreviation **AJ**).

Campsites, both privately and municipally run, are generally excellent, with good facilities for small children. They are very reasonably priced.

If you have not booked in advance, the best bet is to head for the local tourist office (**Office de tourisme** or **Syndicat d'initiative**) where you will find all the information on accommodation options in the area.

Note that in order to use a British electrical appliance, you will need a continental adaptor, available in electrical shops in the UK.

## The basics

| | |
|---|---|
| **air conditioning** | climatisation *klee-ma-tee-zas-yON* |
| **bath** | baignoire *ben-war* |
| **bathroom** | salle de bains *sal duh bAN* |

| | |
|---|---|
| **bathroom with shower** | salle de bains avec douche *sal duh bAN avek doosh* |
| **bed** | lit *lee* |
| **bed and breakfast** | chambre d'hôtes *shON-bruh doht* |
| **campsite** | camping *kON-peeng* |
| **caravan** | caravane *ka-ra-van* |
| **double bed** | lit double *lee doobl* |
| **double room** | chambre double *shON-bruh doobl* |
| **en-suite bathroom** | chambre avec salle de bains *shONbr avek sal duh bAN* |
| **family room** | chambre familiale *shON-bruh fa-meel-yal* |
| **flat** | appartement *a-par-tuh-mON* |
| **full-board** | pension complète *pONs-yON kON-plet* |
| **fully inclusive** | tout compris *too kON-pree* |
| **half-board** | demi-pension *duh-mee-pONs-yON* |
| **holiday cottage** | gîte *zheet* |
| **hotel** | hôtel *oh-tel* |
| **rent** | loyer *lwa-yay* |
| **satellite television** | télévision par satellite *tay-lay-veez-yON par sa-tay-leet* |
| **self-catering accommodation** | location *loh-kas-yON* |
| **shower** | douche *doosh* |
| **single bed** | lit pour une personne *lee poor Un per-son* |
| **single room** | chambre individuelle/simple *shONbr AN-dee-vee-dU-el/sANpl* |
| **tenant** | locataire *loh-ka-ter* |
| **tent** | tente *tONt* |
| **toilets** | toilettes *twa-let* |
| **youth hostel** | auberge de jeunesse *oh-berzh duh zhuh-nes* |
| **to book** | réserver *ray-zer-vay* |
| **to rent** | louer *loo-ay* |

## Expressing yourself

**I have a reservation**
j'ai fait une réservation
*zhay fay Un ray-zer-vas-yON*

**the name's …**
mon nom est …
*mON nON ay …*

34

**do you take credit cards?**
est-ce qu'on peut payer par carte ?
*ess-kON puh pay-yay par kart ?*

## Understanding

| | |
|---|---|
| **accueil** | reception |
| **arrhes** | deposit |
| **chambres libres** | vacancies |
| **complet** | full |
| **privé** | private |
| **réception** | reception |
| **sdb** (= **s**alle de **b**ains) | bathroom |
| **toilettes** | toilets |

# HOTELS

### Expressing yourself

**do you have any vacancies?**
est-ce qu'il vous reste une chambre de libre ?
*ess keel voo rest Un shONbr duh leebr ?*

**how much is a double room per night?**
combien coûte une chambre double ?
*kON-byAN koot Un shON-bruh doobl ?*

**I'd like to book a double room/a single room**
je voudrais réserver une chambre double/chambre individuelle
*zhuh voo-dray ray-zer-vay Un shON-bruh doobl/shONbr AN-dee-vee-dU-el*

**for three nights**
pour trois nuits
*poor trwa nwee*

**would it be possible to stay an extra night?**
serait-il possible de rester une nuit de plus ?
*suh-ray-teel poh-seebl duh res-tay Un nwee duh plUs ?*

**do you have any rooms available for tonight?**
est-ce qu'il vous reste une chambre de libre pour cette nuit ?
*ess keel voo rest Un shONbr duh leebr poor set nwee ?*

**do you have any family rooms?**
avez-vous des chambres familiales ?
*avay-voo day shONbr fa-meel-yal ?*

**would it be possible to add an extra bed?**
serait-il possible d'avoir un lit supplémentaire ?
*suh-ray-teel poh-seebl dav-war AN lee sU-play-mON-ter ?*

**could I see the room first?**
est-ce que je pourrais d'abord voir la chambre ?
*ess-kuh zhuh poo-ray da-bor vwar la shONbr ?*

**do you have anything bigger/quieter?**
avez-vous quelque chose de plus grand/calme ?
*avay-voo kel-kuh-shohz duh plU grON/kalm ?*

**that's fine, I'll take it**
c'est bon, je la prends
*say bON, zhuh la prON*

**is there a lift?**
y a-t-il un ascenseur ?
*ya-teel AN a-sON-suhr ?*

**could you recommend any other hotels?**
pourriez-vous me recommander d'autres hôtels ?
*poor-yay-voo muh ruh-koh-mON-day doh-truhz ohtel ?*

**is breakfast included?**
le petit déjeuner est-il compris ?
*luh puh-tee day-zhuh-nay ay-teel kON-pree ?*

**what time do you serve breakfast?**
à quelle heure est servi le petit déjeuner ?
*a kel uhr ay ser-vee luh puh-tee day-zhuh-nay ?*

**is the hotel near the centre of town?**
est-ce que l'hôtel est près du centre ?
*ess-kuh lohtel ay pray dU sONtr ?*

**what time will the room be ready?**
à quelle heure la chambre sera-t-elle prête ?
*a kel uhr la shONbr suhra-tel pret ?*

**the key for room …, please**
la clé de la chambre …, s'il vous plaît
*la klay duh la shONbr …, seel voo play*

**could I have an extra blanket?**
est-ce que je pourrais avoir une couverture en plus ?
*ess-kuh zhuh poo-ray av-war Un koo-ver-tUr ON plUs ?*

**the air conditioning isn't working**
la climatisation ne marche pas
*la klee-ma-tee-zas-yON nuh marsh pa*

## Understanding

**je regrette mais nous sommes complets**
I'm sorry, but we're full

**il ne nous reste qu'une chambre double**
we only have a double room available

**c'est pour combien de nuits ?**    **à quel nom, s'il vous plaît ?**
how many nights is it for?      what's your name, please?

**les chambres sont disponibles à partir de midi**
check-in is from midday

**la chambre doit être libérée avant midi**
you have to check out before midday

**le petit déjeuner est servi dans le restaurant entre 8 et 10h**
breakfast is served in the restaurant between 8am and 10am

**votre chambre n'est pas encore prête**
your room isn't ready yet

**vous pouvez laisser vos bagages ici**
you can leave your bags here

# YOUTH HOSTELS

## Expressing yourself

**do you have space for two people for tonight?**
est-ce qu'il vous reste de la place pour deux personnes pour cette nuit ?
*ess-keel voo rest duh la plas poor duh per-son poor set nwee ?*

**we've booked two beds for three nights**
on a réservé pour deux personnes pour trois nuits
*ON a ray-zer-vay poor duh per-son poor trwa nwee*

**could I leave my backpack at reception?**
est-ce que je peux laisser mon sac à dos à la réception ?
*ess-kuh zhuh puh lay-say mON sak a-doh a la ray-seps-yoN ?*

**do you have somewhere we could leave our bikes?**
est-ce qu'il y a un endroit où on pourrait laisser nos vélos ?
*ess-keel ya AN ON-drwa oo ON poo-ray lay-say noh vay-loh ?*

**I'll come back for it around 7 o'clock**
je viendrais le chercher vers sept heures
*zhuh vyAN-dray luh sher-shay ver set uhr*

**there's no hot water**
il n'y a pas d'eau chaude
*eel nya pa doh shohd*

**the sink's blocked**
l'évier est bouché
*lay-vyay ay blo-kay*

## Understanding

est-ce que vous avez une carte de membre ?
do you have a membership card?

les draps sont fournis
bed linen is provided

l'auberge rouvre à six heures
the hostel reopens at 6pm

# SELF-CATERING

## Expressing yourself

**we're looking for somewhere to rent near a town**
nous cherchons une location à proximité d'une ville
*noo sher-shON Un loh-kas-yON a prok-see-mee-tay dUn veel*

**where do we pick up/leave the keys?**
où doit-on prendre/laisser les clés ?
*oo dwat-ON prONdr/lay-say lay klay ?*

**is electricity included in the price?**
l'électricité est-elle comprise dans le prix ?
*lay-lek-tree-see-tay ayt-el kON-preez dON luh pree ?*

**are bed linen and towels provided?**
les draps et serviettes sont-ils fournis ?
*lay dra ay serv-yet sON-teel foor-nee ?*

**is there a pool?**
y a-t-il une piscine ?
*ya-teel Un pee-seen ?*

**is a car necessary?**
faut-il avoir une voiture ?
*foh-teel av-war Un wa-tUr ?*

**is the accommodation suitable for elderly people?**
la location conviendrait-elle à des personnes âgées ?
*la loh-kas-yON kON-vyAN-dret-el a day per-son za-zhay ?*

**where is the nearest supermarket?**
où est le supermarché le plus proche ?
*oo ay luh sU-per-mar-shay luh plU prosh ?*

## Understanding

**veuillez laisser la maison dans l'état où vous l'avez trouvée**
please leave the house clean and tidy when you leave

**la maison est entièrement meublée**
the house is fully furnished

**tout est inclus dans le prix**
everything is included in the price

**il est indispensable d'avoir une voiture dans cette région**
you really need a car in this part of the country

# CAMPING

## Expressing yourself

**is there a campsite near here?**
est-ce qu'il y a un camping par ici ?
*ess-keel ya AN kON-peeng par ee-see ?*

**I'd like to book a space for a four-person tent for three nights**
je voudrais réserver un emplacement pour une tente de quatre
personnes pour trois jours
*zhuh voo-dray ray-zer-vay AN ON-plas-mON poor Un tONt duh kat per-son
poor trwa zhoor*

**how much is it a night?**
ça coûte combien par jour ?
*sa koot kON-byAN par zhoor ?*

**where is the shower block?**
où sont les douches ?
*oo sON lay doosh ?*

**can we pay, please? we were at space ...**
nous venons régler – nous étions à l'emplacement ...
*noo vuh-nON ray-glay – nooz ay-tyON a lON-plas-mON ...*

## Understanding

**c'est ... par personne et par jour**
it's ... per person per night

**n'hésitez pas à demander si vous avez besoin de quoique ce soit**
if you need anything, just come and ask

Everybody knows that when you go to France there is no problem about being able to eat well. Restaurants (**restaurants**), even in big cities, vary from the internationally renowned to small family-run establishments. **Brasseries** and **bistrots** are generally modest but can also be quite grand – and expensive. You will always find the menu displayed outside so you can check out what type of food is on offer and whether the prices suit your budget. In a modest brasserie or restaurant you will find a variety of simple starters, main courses and desserts along with the day's specials (**plats du jour**).

Wherever you are, the best-value option is often to choose a set menu (**menu**). If you opt for a three-course menu, you usually have the choice between cheese or dessert. Cheese is served before dessert. You can also choose from the **à la carte** menu where each dish is priced separately. In rural areas, look out for menus offering local specialities (**menu terroir**). A simple menu for children (**menu d'enfant**) is usually available.

In many cafés and most brasseries you can find quick snacks (**casse-croûte**), sandwiches and salads.

Lunch is still regarded as the important meal in many contexts in France. Service begins at midday. In most restaurants you will not be served after 2pm. In the evening, service will begin around 7pm. In rural areas, service will stop at around 9pm whilst the big brasseries in cities serve until late in the evening.

Pizza and hamburger restaurants can be found almost everywhere. France also offers a variety of ethnic food, especially North African, Vietnamese and Cambodian.

Wherever you eat, as much bread and tap water as you want is provided free of charge. In more modest restaurants, you can order a jug (**pichet**) of the house wine. You can choose the quantity. You will often be asked whether you want a pre-meal drink (**apéritif**). Popular choices are Pernod and **kir** (white wine flavoured with blackcurrant liqueur). Service is always included but a tip according to quality of service is expected.

Cafés are usually open from early in the morning until late at night (though they generally close fairly early in rural areas). Always sit down and wait for table service. Note that if you order a coffee (**un café**) this will always be a small expresso without milk. A coffee with milk is **un café crème**. Cafés usually serve a variety of alcoholic drinks, including both bottled and draught lager. To order the latter ask for **un demi** or **une pression** (a little less than a British half). The age limit for drinking alcohol is 18.

## The basics

| | |
|---|---|
| **beer** | bière *byer* |
| **bill** | addition *a-dees-yON* |
| **black coffee** | café *ka-fay* |
| **bottle** | bouteille *boo-tey* |
| **bread** | pain *pAN* |
| **breakfast** | petit déjeuner *puh-tee day-zhuh-nay* |
| **coffee** | café *ka-fay* |
| **Coke®** | coca *ko-ka* |
| **dessert** | dessert *day-ser* |
| **dinner** | dîner *dee-nay* |
| **fruit juice** | jus de fruit *zhU duh frwee* |
| **lemonade** | limonade *lee-moh-nad* |
| **lunch** | déjeuner *day-zhuh-nay* |
| **main course** | plat (principal) *pla (prAN-see-pal)* |
| **menu** | carte *kart* |
| **mineral water** | eau minérale *oh mee-nay-ral* |
| **red wine** | vin rouge *vAN roozh* |
| **rosé wine** | rosé *roh-zay* |
| **salad** | salade *sa-lad* |
| **sandwich** | sandwich *sON-dweech* |
| **service** | service *ser-vees* |
| **sparkling water** | eau gazeuse *oh ga-zuhz* |
| **starter** | entrée *ON-tray* |
| **still water** | eau plate *oh plat* |
| **tea** | thé *tay* |

EATING AND DRINKING

| tip | pourboire *poor-bwar* |
|---|---|
| water | eau *oh* |
| white coffee | café crème *ka-fay krem* |
| white wine | vin blanc *vAN blON* |
| wine | vin *vAN* |
| wine list | liste des vins *leest day vAN* |
| to eat | manger *mON-zhay* |
| to have breakfast | prendre le petit déjeuner *prONdr luh puh-tee day-zhuh-nay* |
| to have dinner | dîner *dee-nay* |
| to have lunch | déjeuner *day-zhuh-nay* |
| to order | commander *koh-mON-day* |

## Expressing yourself

**shall we go and have something to eat?**
on va manger un bout ?
*ON va mON-zhay AN boo ?*

**do you want to go for a drink?**
ça te dit d'aller boire un verre ?
*sa tuh dee dalay bwar AN ver ?*

**can you recommend a good restaurant?**
est-ce vous pouvez me recommander un bon restaurant ?
*ess-kuh voo poo-vay muh ruh-koh-mON-day AN bON res-toh-rON ?*

**I'm not very hungry**
je n'ai pas très faim
*zhuh nay pa tray fAN*

**excuse me!** (to call the waiter)
s'il vous plaît !
*seel voo play !*

**cheers!**
tchin-tchin !
*cheen-cheen !*

**that was lovely**
c'était très bien
*say-tay tray byAN*

**could you bring us an ashtray, please?**
s'il vous plaît, est-ce qu'on pourrait avoir un cendrier ?
*seel voo play, ess-kON poo-ray avwar AN sON-dree-ay ?*

**where are the toilets, please?**
excusez-moi, où sont les toilettes ?
*ek-skU-zay mwa, oo sON lay twa-let ?*

EATING AND DRINKING

43

## Understanding

| | |
|---|---|
| à emporter | takeaway |
| casse-croûte | snack |
| maison | home-made |
| menu | set menu |
| plat du jour | today's special |
| spécialités de la maison | our specialities |
| sur place | eating in |

# RESERVING A TABLE

### Expressing yourself

**I'd like to reserve a table for tomorrow evening**
je voudrais réserver une table pour demain soir
*zhuh voo-dray ray-zer-vay Un tabl poor duh-mAN swar*

**for two people**
pour deux
*poor duh*

**around 8 o'clock**
vers huit heures
*ver weet uhr*

**do you have a table available any earlier than that?**
est-ce que vous avez une table de libre plus tôt ?
*ess-kuh vooz avay Un tabl duh leebr plU toh ?*

**I've reserved a table – the name's ...**
j'ai réservé au nom de ...
*zhay ray-zer-vay oh nON duh ...*

### Understanding

**réservé**
reserved

**pour quelle heure ?**
for what time?

**c'est à quel nom ?**
what's the name?

**pour combien de personnes ?**
for how many people?

**vous avez réservé ?**
do you have a reservation?

**cette table dans le coin vous convient ?**
is that table in the corner OK for you?

**je regrette mais nous sommes complet**
I'm afraid we're full at the moment

# ORDERING FOOD

**yes, we're ready to order**
oui, on a choisi
*wee, ON a shwa-zee*

**I'll have that**
je vais prendre ça
*zhuh vay prONdr sa*

**no, could you give us a few more minutes?**
non, donnez-nous encore un petit moment
*nON, do-nay noo ON-kor AN puh-tee moh-mON*

**could I have …?**
est-ce que je pourrais avoir … ?
*ess-kuh zhuh poo-ray av-war … ?*

**I'd like …**
je voudrais …
*zhuh voo-dray …*

**I'm not sure, what's "sole meunière"?**
je ne suis pas sûr, qu'est-ce que c'est "sole meunière" ?
*zhuh nuh swee pa sUr, kess-kuh say sol muh-nyer ?*

**does it come with vegetables?**
est-ce que c'est servi avec des légumes ?
*ess-kuh say ser-vee avek day lay-gUm ?*

**what are today's specials?**
quels sont les plats du jour ?
*kel sON lay pla dU zhoor ?*

**and a bottle of red/white wine**
et une bouteille de vin rouge/blanc
*ay Un boo-tey duh vAN roozh/blON*

**what desserts do you have?**
qu'est-ce que vous avez comme desserts ?
*kess-kuh vooz avay kom day-ser ?*

**that's for me**
c'est pour moi
*say poor mwa*

**could we have some water, please**
une carafe d'eau, s'il vous plaît
*Un ka-raf doh seel voo play*

EATING AND DRINKING

45

**this isn't what I ordered, I wanted …**
ce n'est pas ce que j'ai commandé, j'avais demandé …
*suh nay pa suh kuh zhay koh-mON-day, zhavay duh-mON-day …*

**could we have some more bread, please?**
est-ce qu'on pourrait avoir un peu plus de pain, s'il vous plaît ?
*ess-kON poo-ray av-war AN puh plUs duh pAN, seel voo play ?*

**could you bring us another jug of water, please?**
est-ce que vous pourriez nous apporter une autre carafe d'eau, s'il vous plaît ?
*ess-kuh voo poor-yay nooz a-por-tay Un oh-truh ka-raf doh, seel voo play ?*

## Understanding

**fromage ou dessert au choix**    choice of cheese or dessert

**vous avez choisi ?**
are you ready to order?

**je vous laisse choisir et je reviens**
I'll leave you to choose and I'll come back in a minute

**désolé, il ne reste plus de …**
I'm sorry, we don't have any … left

**vous le voulez avec des frites ou de la salade ?**
would you like that with chips or salad?

**qu'est-ce que vous voulez boire ?**
what would you like to drink?

**est-ce que vous voulez un dessert ? un café ?**
would you like dessert or coffee?

**ça a été ?**
was everything OK?

# BARS AND CAFÉS

## Expressing yourself

**I'd like…**
je voudrais …
*zhuh voo-dray …*

**a Coke®**
un Coca®
*AN koka*

**a diet Coke®**
un Coca® light
*AN koka la-eet*

**a glass of red/white wine**
un verre de vin rouge/blanc
*AN ver duh vAN roozh/blON*

**a black/white coffee**
un café/café crème
*AN ka-fay/ka-fay krem*

**a cup of tea**
un thé
*AN tay*

**a coffee and a croissant**
un café et un croissant
*AN ka-fay ay AN krwa-sON*

**a cup of hot chocolate**
un chocolat chaud
*AN shoh-koh-la shoh*

**the same again, please**
la même chose, s'il vous plaît
*la mem shohz, seel voo play*

---

### Some informal expressions

**j'ai un petit creux** I'm a bit peckish
**je crève de faim** I'm starving
**bouffe** food
**bouffer** to eat
**picoler** to booze
**prendre une cuite** to get plastered
**avoir la gueule de bois** to have a hangover

---

## Understanding

**sans alcool**
non-alcoholic

**c'est un espace non-fumeur**
this is a non-smoking area

**qu'est-ce que vous prendrez ?**
what would you like?

**je vais devoir encaisser, s'il vous plaît**
could I ask you to pay now, please?

# THE BILL

### Expressing yourself

**the bill, please**
l'addition s'il vous plaît
*la-dees-yON seel voo play*

**how much do I owe you?**
je vous dois combien ?
*zhuh voo dwa kON-byAN ?*

**do you take credit cards?**
est-ce qu'on peut payer par carte ?
*ess-kON puh pay-yay par kart ?*

**I think there's a mistake in the bill**
je crois qu'il y a une erreur dans l'addition
*zhuh krwa keel ya Un e-ruhr dON la-dees-yON*

**is service included?**
le service est-il compris ?
*luh ser-vees ay-teel kON-pree ?*

### Understanding

**vous réglez tout ensemble ?**
are you all paying together?

**oui, le service est compris**
yes, service is included

# FOOD AND DRINK

## Understanding

| | |
|---|---|
| **à l'étouffée** | braised |
| **à point** | medium rare |
| **bien cuit** | well done |
| **bouilli** | boiled |
| **braisé** | braised |
| **cru** | raw; *(milk)* unpasteurized |
| **cuit au feu de bois** | cooked in a wood-fired oven |
| **doré** | lightly browned |
| **en morceaux** | chopped |
| **en tranches** | sliced |
| **faire bouillir** | to boil |
| **faire chauffer** | to heat |
| **faire gratiner** | to brown (under the grill or in the oven) |
| **farci** | stuffed |
| **fondu** | melted |
| **frit** | fried |
| **fumé** | smoked |
| **grillé** | grilled |
| **pané** | breaded |
| **poché** | poached |
| **poêlé** | pan-fried |
| **râpé** | grated |
| **rôti** | roast |
| **saignant** | rare |
| **salé** | salted |
| **sauté** | sautéed |
| **séché** | dried |
| **vapeur, à la vapeur** | steamed |

♦ **petits déjeuners, goûters** breakfasts, snacks

| | |
|---|---|
| **beurre** | butter |
| **biscotte** | piece of toasted bread (often sold in packets) |
| **brioche** | brioche, bun |

| | |
|---|---|
| **café** | coffee |
| **café au lait** | white coffee |
| **café crème** | white coffee |
| **chausson aux pommes** | apple turnover |
| **chocolat chaud** | hot chocolate |
| **confiture** | jam |
| **croissant (au beurre)** | croissant (made with pure butter) |
| **gelée de myrtilles** | bilberry jelly |
| **jus de fruit** | fruit juice |
| **madeleine** | small sponge cake |
| **miel** | honey |
| **pain** | bread |
| **pain au chocolat** | chocolate-filled pastry |
| **pain au lait** | milk roll |
| **pain aux raisins** | raisin and custard pastry |
| **pain perdu** | French toast |
| **quatre-quarts** | rich sponge cake |
| **tartine** | piece of bread and butter |
| **tartine grillée** | piece of toast |
| **thé** | tea |

### ◆ sur le pouce snacks

| | |
|---|---|
| **croque-madame** | toasted ham and cheese sandwich topped with a fried egg |
| **croque-monsieur** | toasted ham and cheese sandwich |
| **omelette (nature)** | (plain) omelette |

### ◆ apéritifs, amuse-gueule cocktail snacks and nibbles

| | |
|---|---|
| **bouchées à la reine** | vol-au-vent |
| **cacahouètes** | peanuts |
| **chips** | crisps |
| **feuilletés** | puff pastry nibbles |
| **œufs de caille** | quails' eggs |
| **olives** | olives |
| **petits gâteaux salés** | savoury biscuits |
| **saucisson** | French salami |
| **toasts** | small pieces of bread with a savoury topping |

A typical French lunch or dinner consists of a starter (**entrée**), a main course (**plat principal**), cheese (**fromage**) and dessert (**dessert**). At home families traditionally ate a big lunch and had a lighter meal or snack in the evening but this now varies greatly according to ways of life. Sunday lunch is often a big occasion when people invite friends or family for a lengthy, lavish meal.

### ◆ entrées starters

| | |
|---|---|
| **assiette de charcuterie** | mixed platter of salami, ham, pâté etc |
| **assiette de crudités** | platter of assorted salads |
| **bisque de homard** | lobster bisque |
| **carottes râpées** | grated carrot salad |
| **crème de champignons** | mushroom soup |
| **cuisses de grenouille** | frogs' legs |
| **escargots à la bourguignonne** | snails stuffed with garlic butter |
| **foie gras** | foie gras (goose or duck liver, often as a pâté) |
| **gâteau de foie de volaille** | chicken-liver soufflé |
| **œufs durs farcis** | stuffed eggs |
| **pâté de campagne** | coarsely textured pork-based pâté |
| **poireaux à la vinaigrette** | leeks with vinaigrette dressing |
| **rillettes de canard/porc** | potted duck/pork |
| **salade composée** | mixed salad |
| **salade de gésiers de canard confits** | green salad with duck gizzards |
| **salade de lentilles** | lentil salad |
| **salade de magret de canard** | smoked duck breast salad |
| **salade lyonnaise** | green salad with bacon pieces, poached egg and croûtons |
| **salade niçoise** | mixed salad with tuna and anchovies |
| **soufflé au fromage** | cheese soufflé |
| **soupe au pistou** | Mediterranean vegetable soup flavoured with pesto |

| | |
|---|---|
| **soupe à l'oignon** | French onion soup |
| **soupe de poisson** | fish soup |
| **taboulé** | tabbouleh (couscous salad with tomato, lemon, herbs and olive oil) |
| **terrine de lapin/poisson** | rabbit/fish terrine |
| **velouté d'asperges** | cream of asparagus |
| **velouté de volaille** | chicken soup |

### ◆ poissons et fruits de mer fish and shellfish

| | |
|---|---|
| **darne de saumon** | salmon steak |
| **daurade au four** | oven-roasted sea bream |
| **homard à l'américaine** | lobster cooked with white wine, brandy, and tomatoes |
| **moules à la vapeur** | steamed mussels |
| **moules marinières** | mussels cooked with shallots and white wine |
| **plateau de fruits de mer** | seafood platter |
| **sardines grillées** | grilled sardines |
| **sole meunière** | Dover sole pan-fried in butter |

### ◆ volaille poultry

| | |
|---|---|
| **canard à l'orange** | duck with orange sauce |
| **confit de canard/d'oie** | preserved duck/goose |
| **coq au vin** | cockerel cooked in red wine |
| **foie gras poêlé** | pan-fried fresh foie gras |
| **fricassée de poulet** | chicken with mushrooms in a cream sauce |
| **pintade aux choux** | guinea fowl with cabbage |
| **poule au pot** | boiling fowl poached with a variety of vegetables (the cooking liquid is usually served first as a soup) |
| **poule au riz** | boiling fowl poached with rice |
| **poulet à l'estragon** | tarragon chicken |
| **poulet basquaise** | chicken sautéed with tomatoes and green peppers |

### ◆ gibier game

| | |
|---|---|
| **civet de lièvre** | hare cooked with the blood and red wine and/or port |
| **lapin à la moutarde** | rabbit cooked in mustard and white wine |
| **magret de canard** | duck breast |
| **poulet rôti** | roast chicken |
| **rôti de dinde** | roast turkey |
| **rôti de chevreuil** | roast venison |

### ◆ viandes meat

| | |
|---|---|
| **blanquette de veau** | veal in a creamy sauce |
| **bœuf bourguignon** | rich, winey beef stew |
| **bœuf en daube** | beef marinated and cooked slowly in red wine |
| **boudin aux pommes** | black pudding with baked or fried apples |
| **côtes/côtelettes d'agneau** | lamb chops |
| **côte de porc/veau** | pork/veal chop |
| **escalope de veau panée** | breaded veal escalope |
| **foie de veau en persillade** | pan-fried veal liver with parsley and garlic |
| **gigot d'agneau (au four)** | roast leg of lamb |
| **navarin d'agneau** | lamb sautéed with spring vegetables |
| **pavé de bœuf** | thick steak |
| **ris de veau** | veal sweetbreads |
| **rôti de porc aux pruneaux** | roast pork stuffed with prunes |
| **rôti de veau** | roast veal |
| **steak au poivre** | pepper steak |
| **steak tartare** | steak tartare (raw, finely minced steak with seasoning) |
| **tripes à la mode de Caen** | tripe cooked in cider and Calvados |

### ◆ accompagnements accompaniments

| | |
|---|---|
| **épinards à la crème** | spinach with cream |
| **gratin dauphinois** | sliced potatoes baked in cream |
| **gratin de macaronis** | macaroni cheese |

FOOD AND DRINK

53

| | |
|---|---|
| **jardinière de légumes** | mixed vegetables |
| **pommes boulangères** | potatoes cooked under a roast |
| **pommes dauphine** | lightly battered potato balls |
| **pommes rissolées** | sautéed cubed potatoes |
| **ratatouille** | stew of aubergines, peppers, courgettes and tomatoes |
| **riz basquaise** | rice pilaf with tomatoes and green peppers |

### ◆ plats uniques composite dishes

| | |
|---|---|
| **bouillabaisse** | Mediterranean fish stew |
| **cassoulet** | casserole of preserved goose, Toulouse sausage and white beans |
| **choucroute garnie** | pickled cabbage with various sausages, salt pork etc |
| **endives au jambon** | chicory wrapped in ham and baked in a creamy sauce |
| **fondue bourguignonne** | fondue consisting of a pan of hot oil in which you cook your own cubes of meat and select from a variety of sauces |
| **fondue savoyarde** | cheese fondue |
| **hachis Parmentier** | shepherd's pie |
| **moules-frites** | steamed mussels with French fries |
| **petit salé aux lentilles** | salt bacon cooked with lentils, carrots and onions |
| **pot-au-feu** | meat boiled with a variety of vegetables |
| **raclette** | dish consisting of cheese melted on a grill at the table and served with steamed potatoes and cured ham |

## ◆ fromage cheese

France boasts an immense variety of cheeses of every type imaginable. Most regions have their own specialities and it is worth seeking these out in markets and in restaurants. In restaurants you are sometimes given the choice between fromage frais (**fromage blanc** in France) and a selection of cheeses. Cheese is always eaten before dessert.

## ◆ desserts et pâtisseries desserts and pastries

| | |
|---|---|
| **baba au rhum** | rum baba |
| **bavarois** | creamy mousse, often containing fruit |
| **beignets** | fritters |
| **bûche de Noël** | chocolate Yule log |
| **charlotte aux fruits rouges** | red fruit mousse sourrounded by sponge fingers |
| **clafoutis** | fruit baked in a sweet batter |
| **compote de pommes** | apple puree |
| **crêpe Suzette** | crêpes flambéed in Cointreau |
| **far breton** | rich Breton prune cake |
| **flan** | custard tart |
| **galette des Rois** | puff-pastry cake filled with almond paste, traditionally eaten at Epiphany (6 January). It comes with a cardboard crown to be worn by the person who finds the little figure in the cake (la fève, so called because originally a bean was used) |
| **gâteau de riz** | caramelized rice pudding |
| **gaufre** | waffle |
| **glace** | ice cream |
| **île flottante** | whipped egg-white poached in vanilla custard |
| **macédoine/salade de fruits** | fruit salad |
| **mille-feuille** | puff pastry layered with vanilla custard |
| **mousse au chocolat** | chocolate mousse |

| poire Belle-Hélène | pears with ice cream and hot chocolate sauce |
| pomme au four | baked apple |
| tarte au citron | lemon tart |
| tarte aux noix/framboises | walnut/raspberry tart |
| tarte Tatin | caramelized upside-down apple tart |
| vacherin | ice cream and meringue cake |

◆ **boissons** drinks

France produces a huge variety of excellent wines and you will not usually find wines from other countries in shops or on wine lists. Even very modest cafés will always offer wine with food. There are a number of French lagers and bottled light stouts available and cafés and brasseries will have draught lager. You can also find various types of beer from other countries, though UK-type draught beer and draught Guinness are generally only available in English and Irish pubs, of which there are many in bigger cities.

Normandy is famed for its cider. When accompanying a meal, especially in a pancake restaurant (**crêperie**), cider is often served in earthenware bowls.

People will often have a pre-meal drink (**apéritif**) and you will generally be offered one in a restaurant or if you are invited to eat in a French home. It is also quite common to invite friends in just for apéritifs and nibbles. Common apéritifs are whisky (**whisky**), port (**porto**), various sweet wines (**vins doux**), aniseed alcohols (**pastis**) and **kir** (white wine with blackcurrant liqueur).

Coffee is usually drunk after a meal. In someone's home you may be offered a herbal tea (**tisane**) as an alternative, particularly in the evening.

After-dinner drinks are always on offer in restaurants and vary little from those available in the UK, though fruit alcohols, often produced by small local distillers, are particularly prized in France.

# FOOD AND DRINK GLOSSARY

**abricot** apricot
**agneau** lamb
**aigre-doux** sweet-and-sour
**ail** garlic
**aïoli** garlic mayonnaise
**amande** almond
**ananas** pineapple
**anchois** anchovy
**anguille** eel
**aneth** dill
**arête** fishbone
**artichaut** artichoke
**asperges** asparagus
**assiette** plate
**aubergine** aubergine
**avocat** avocado
**bacon** smoked back bacon
**banane** banana
**bar** sea bass
**basilic** basil
**betterave** beetroot
**beurre doux/demi-sel** unsalted/
salted butter
**bière** beer
**bifteck** steak
**bigorneaux** winkles
**blanc de poulet** chicken breast
**blettes** Swiss chard
**boîte de conserve** can of food
**boudin blanc** white pudding
(made with chicken or veal)
**boudin noir** black pudding
**boulettes** meatballs
**brochet** pike
**brochette** kebab
**brocoli** broccoli

**brugnon** nectarine
**caille** quail
**cabillaud** cod
**calamar** squid
**canard** duck
**cannelle** cinnamon
**câpres** capers
**carotte** carrot
**cassis** blackcurrants
**céleri** celery
**cèpes** ceps
**cerises** cherries
**champignons** mushrooms
**champignons de Paris** button
mushrooms
**chapon** capon
**châtaigne** chestnut
**chevreuil** venison
**chips** (potato) crisps
**chocolat** chocolate
**chou** cabbage
**chou-fleur** cauliflower
**choux de Bruxelles** Brussels
sprouts
**ciboulette** chives
**cidre** cider
**citron** lemon
**citron vert** lime
**citrouille** pumpkin
**clous de girofle** cloves
**cœurs d'artichaut** artichoke
hearts
**cognac** brandy
**colin** hake, coley
**concombre** cucumber
**congelé** frozen

**conservateur** preservative
**coquilles Saint-Jacques** scallops
**cornichons** gherkins
**côtelette** cutlet
**crabe** crab
**crème Chantilly** sweetened whipped cream
**crème fraîche** thick, slightly soured fresh cream
**crème pâtissière** confectioner's custard
**crêpe (de froment)** (wholewheat) pancake
**cresson** cress
**crevettes** prawns
**cuillère** spoon, spoonful
**cuillère à café** teaspoon, teaspoonful
**cuillère à soupe** soup spoon, tablespoonful
**cuillérée** teaspoonful
**cuisse de poulet** chicken leg
**daurade** sea bream
**déjeuner** lunch
**dessert** dessert
**dinde** turkey
**échalote** shallot
**écrevisses** crayfish
**édulcorant** sweetener
**églefin** haddock
**en conserve** tinned, preserved
**endives** chicory
**épice** spice
**épinards** spinach
**estragon** tarragon
**faisan** pheasant
**farine** flour
**fenouil** fennel
**fèves** broad beans

**figue** fig
**filet** fillet
**flétan** halibut
**foie** liver
**four** oven
**fraises** strawberries
**framboises** raspberries
**frites** French fries, chips
**fromage** cheese
**fromage blanc** fromage frais (thick yoghurt)
**fruits de mer** seafood
**fruits rouges** summer fruits (raspberry, strawberry, redcurrant etc)
**galette (de blé noir/de sarrasin)** buckwheat pancake
**garniture** garnish, accompaniment
**gâteau** cake
**girolles** a type of wild mushroom
**glace** ice cream
**gratin** a dish, usually vegetable or fish, cooked and browned in a sauce in the oven
**groseilles** redcurrants
**haddock** smoked haddock
**hareng** herring
**hareng fumé** smoked herring
**haricots verts** green beans
**huile** oil
**huile d'olive** olive oil
**huître** oyster
**jambon blanc, jambon cuit** (cooked) ham
**jambon cru/du pays/de Bayonne** cured raw ham
**lait** milk
**lait cru** unpasteurized milk
**lait demi-écrémé** semi-skimmed milk

**lait écrémé** skimmed milk
**lait entier** full-cream milk
**laitue** round lettuce
**langouste** rock lobster
**lapin** rabbit
**lard fumé/salé** smoked/ unsmoked bacon
**lardons** small strips of bacon
**laurier** bayleaves
**lentilles** lentils
**lièvre** hare
**limande** lemon sole
**lotte** monkfish
**maïs** sweetcorn
**maquereau** mackerel
**menthe** mint
**merguez** spicy lamb or beef sausages
**merlan** whiting
**merlu** hake
**miel** honey
**morue** salt cod
**moules** mussels
**moutarde** mustard
**mûr** ripe
**mûres** blackberries
**myrtilles** bilberries
**navet** turnip
**noisettes** hazelnuts
**noix** walnuts
**noix de coco** coconut
**noix de muscade** nutmeg
**œuf** egg
**œuf à la coque** boiled egg
**œuf dur** hard-boiled egg
**œuf sur le plat** fried egg
**oignon** onion
**omelette** omelette
**orange** orange

**origan** oregano
**pain** bread
**pain au levain** sourdough bread
**pain au son** bran bread
**pain aux céréales** wholegrain bread
**pain complet** wholemeal bread
**pain de campagne** traditional country bread
**pain de mie** sliced bread
**pain de seigle** rye bread
**palourdes** clams
**parfum** flavour
**pastèque** watermelon
**pâte de coings** quince paste
**pâtes** pasta
**pêche** peach
**perdrix** partridge
**persil** parsley
**petit déjeuner** breakfast
**petits pois** peas
**pigeonneau** young pigeon
**pintade** guinea fowl
**piquant** spicy
**plat garni** dish served with vegetables
**plat principal** main dish
**poêle** frying pan
**poire** pear
**poireau** leek
**pois chiches** chickpeas
**poisson** fish
**poivre** pepper
**poivre en grains** peppercorns
**poivron rouge/vert** red/green pepper
**pomme** apple
**pomme de terre** potato
**porc** pork

FOOD AND DRINK

59

**potiron** pumpkin
**poulet** chicken
**prune** plum
**pruneau** prune
**pudding** heavy fruit sponge
**purée** mashed potato
**radis** radish
**ragoût** stew
**raie** skate
**raisin** grapes
**raisins secs** raisins, sultanas
**repas** meal
**riz** rice
**rognons** kidneys
**romarin** rosemary
**rôti** roast
**rouget** red mullet
**safran** saffron
**saindoux** lard
**salé** salted; savoury
**sanglier** wild boar
**sardines** sardines
**sauce** sauce
**sauce béchamel** white sauce
**saucisse** sausage

**saucisson** French salami
**saumon** salmon
**sel** salt
**sirop** fruit cordial, squash
**sole** (Dover) sole
**sucre** sugar
**sucré** sweet
**surgelé** frozen
**truite** trout
**turbot** turbot
**thon** tuna
**thym** thyme
**tisane** herbal tea
**tomate** tomato
**tourte** pie
**tourteau** crab
**truite** trout
**veau** veal
**viande** meat
**viande hachée** minced meat
**vin (blanc/rouge/rosé)** (white/
red/rosé) wine
**vinaigre** vinegar
**vinaigrette** vinaigrette dressing

# GOING OUT

Nightlife in big cities in France is lively and at weekends can go on until the early hours. Bars close at around 2am, while clubs can stay open until at least 5am. A variety of live music can be found in bars and cafés, especially at weekends. In Paris, information on all cultural events and entertainments can be found in "l'Officiel des spectacles" or "Pariscope" (the latter also has information in English). Similar publications can be found in other big cities. These can be bought at newsagents and on news-stands.

If you want to go to the cinema, note that foreign-language films showing at big cinemas are often dubbed into French, while alternative cinemas frequently offer films in the original language, with subtitles in French. These are signalled **V.O.** (**version originale**) in programmes and outside the cinema. Cinemas, theatres and museums generally offer reduced rates for students and people over sixty. Students will be asked to show their student cards and over-sixties to produce evidence of age.

## The basics

| | |
|---|---|
| ballet | ballet *ba-lay* |
| band | groupe *groop* |
| bar | bar *bar* |
| cinema | cinéma *see-nay-ma* |
| circus | cirque *seerk* |
| classical music | musique classique *mU-zeek kla-seek* |
| club | boîte (de nuit) *bwat (duh nwee)* |
| concert | concert *kON-ser* |
| dubbed film | film doublé *feelm doo-blay* |
| festival | festival *fes-tee-val* |
| film | film *feelm* |
| folk music | musique traditionnelle *mU-zeek tra-dees-yoh-nel* |
| jazz | jazz *jaz* |
| modern dance | danse contemporaine *dONs kON-tON-poh-ren* |
| musical | comédie musicale *ko-may-dee mU-zee-kal* |

GOING OUT

| party | *(for a special occasion)* **fête** *fet*, *(in the evening)* |
|---|---|
| | **soirée** *swa-ray* |
| **pop music** | pop *pop* |
| **rock music** | rock *rok* |
| **show** | spectacle *spek-takl* |
| **subtitled film** | film sous-titré *feelm soo-tee-tray* |
| **theatre** | théâtre *tay-ahtr* |
| **ticket** | billet *bee-yay* |
| **to book** | réserver *ray-zer-vay* |
| **to go out** | sortir *sor-teer* |

# SUGGESTIONS AND INVITATIONS

## Expressing yourself

**where can we go?**
où est-ce qu'on pourrait aller ?
*oo ess-kON poo-ray alay ?*

**shall we go for a drink?**
on va prendre un verre ?
*ON va prONdr AN ver ?*

**what do you want to do?**
qu'est-ce que vous avez envie de faire ?
*kess-kuh vooz avay ON-vee duh fer ?*

**what are you doing tonight?**
qu'est-ce que vous faites ce soir ?
*kess-kuh voo fet suh swar ?*

**would you like to …?**
est-ce que vous aimeriez … ?
*ess-kuh vooz ay-muhr-yay … ?*

**do you have plans?**
est-ce que vous avez quelque chose de prévu ?
*ess-kuh vooz avay kel-kuh-shohz duh pray-vU ?*

**we were thinking of going to …**
on pensait aller à …
*ON pON-se alay a …*

**I can't today, but maybe some other time**
aujourd'hui, je ne peux pas, mais peut-être une autre fois
*oh-zhoor-dwee, zhuh nuh puh pa, may puh-tetr Un oh-truh fwa*

**I'd love to**
avec plaisir
*avek play-zeer*

**I'm not sure I can make it**
je ne suis pas sûr de pouvoir
*zhuh nuh swee pa sUr duh poo-vwar*

GOING OUT

# ARRANGING TO MEET

## Expressing yourself

**what time shall we meet?**
on se retrouve à quelle heure ?
*ON suh ruh-troov a kel uhr ?*

**where shall we meet?**
on se retrouve où ?
*ON suh ruh-troov oo ?*

**would it be possible to meet a bit later?**
est-ce qu'il serait possible de se retrouver un peu plus tard ?
*ess-keel suh-ray poh-seebl duh suh ruh-troo-vay AN puh plU tar ?*

**I have to meet … at nine**
j'ai rendez-vous avec … à neuf heures
*zhay rON-day-voo avek … a nuhv uhr*

**I don't know where it is but I'll find it on the map**
je ne sais pas où c'est mais je trouverai sur le plan
*zhuh nuh say pa oo say may zhuh troo-vuh-ray sUr luh plON*

**see you tomorrow night**
à demain soir
*a duh-mAN swar*

**sorry I'm late**
désolé d'être en retard
*day-zoh-lay detr ON ruh-tar*

**I'll meet you later, I have to stop by the hotel first**
je vous retrouverai plus tard, je dois d'abord passer à l'hôtel
*zhuh voo ruh-troo-vuh-ray plU tar, zhuh dwa da-bor pa-say a loh-tel*

**I'll call/text you if there's a change of plan**
je vous appelerai/vous enverrai un SMS s'il y a un changement
*zhuh voo ra-peluh-ray/vooz ON-ve-ray AN ess-em-ess seel ya AN shONzh-mON*

**are you going to eat beforehand?**
est-ce que vous aurez mangé avant ?
*ess kuh vooz oh-ray mON-zhay avON ?*

## Understanding

**ça vous va ?**
is that OK with you?

**on se retrouve là-bas**
I'll meet you there

**je viendrai vous chercher vers huit heures**
I'll come and pick you up about 8

GOING OUT

63

**on peut se retrouver devant …**
we can meet outside …

**je vais vous donner mon numéro pour que vous m'appeliez demain**
I'll give you my number and you can call me tomorrow

---

**Some informal expressions**

**aller boire un coup** to go for a drink
**prendre un pot** to have a drink
**manger un bout** to have a bite to eat
**branché** trendy

---

# FILMS, SHOWS AND CONCERTS

### Expressing yourself

**is there a guide to what's on?**
est-ce qu'il y a un guide des spectacles ?
*ess-keel ya AN geed day spek-takl ?*

**I'd like three tickets for …**
je voudrais trois places pour …
*zhuh voo-dray trwa plass poor …*

**two tickets, please**
deux places, s'il vous plaît
*duh plass, seel voo play*

**it's called …**
ça s'appelle …
*sa sa-pel …*

**I've seen the trailer**
j'ai vu la bande-annonce
*zhay vU la bON-da-nONs*

**what time does it start?**
ça commence à quelle heure ?
*sa koh-mONs a kel uhr ?*

**I'd like to go and see a show**
je voudrais aller voir un spectacle
*zhuh voo-dray alay vwar AN spek-takl*

**I'll find out whether there are still tickets available**
je vais voir s'il reste des places
*zhuh vay vwar seel rest day plass*

**do we need to book in advance?**
est-ce qu'il faut réserver à l'avance ?
*ess-keel foh ray-zer-vay a la-vONs ?*

**how long is it on for?**
ça joue jusqu'à quand ?
*sa zhoo zhUska kON ?*

**are there tickets for another day?**
est-ce qu'il reste des places pour un autre jour ?
*ess-keel rest day plass poor AN ohtr zhoor ?*

**I'd like to go to a bar with some live music**
j'aimerais bien aller écouter de la musique dans un café
*zhay-muh-ray byAN alay ay-koo-tay duh la mUzeek dONz AN ka-fay*

**what sort of music is it?**
c'est quel genre de musique ?
*say kel zhONr duh mU-zeek ?*

**are there any free concerts?**
est-ce qu'il y a des concerts gratuits ?
*ess-keel ya day kON-ser gra-twee ?*

---

## Understanding

| | |
|---|---|
| **guichet** | box office |
| **matinée** | matinée |
| **place sans visibilité** | restricted view |
| **réservations** | bookings |
| **séance** | showing |
| **sortie le …** | on general release from … |
| **VO (sous-titrée)** | subtitles |

**c'est un concert en plein air**
it's an open-air concert

**il y a de très bonnes critiques**
it's had very good reviews

**ça sort la semaine prochaine**
it comes out next week

**ça joue à huit heures à l'UGC**
it's on at 8pm at the UGC

**il n'y a plus de places pour cette séance**
that showing's sold out

**c'est complet jusqu'au …**
it's all booked up until …

**ce n'est pas la peine de réserver**
there's no need to book in advance

**la pièce dure une heure et demie avec entracte**
the play lasts an hour and a half, including the interval

**prière d'éteindre votre portable**
please turn off your mobile phones

# PARTIES AND CLUBS

## Expressing yourself

**I'm having a little leaving party tonight**
je fais une petite fête pour mon départ ce soir
*zhuh fay Un puh-teet fet poor mON day-par suh swar*

**should I bring something to drink?**
est-ce qu'il faut apporter quelque chose à boire ?
*ess-keel foh a-por-tay kel-kuh-shohz a bwar ?*

**we could go to a club afterwards**
on pourrait aller en boîte après
*ON poo-ray alay ON bwat a-pray*

**do you have to pay to get in?**
l'entrée est payante ?
*lON-tray ay pay-yONt ?*

**I have to meet someone inside**
je dois retrouver quelqu'un à l'intérieur
*zhuh dwa ruh-troo-vay kel-kAN a lAN-tayr-yuhr*

**will you let me back in when I come back?**
vous me laisserez entrer quand je reviens ?
*voo muh lay-suh-ray ON-tray kON zhuh ruhv-yAN ?*

**the DJ's really cool**
le DJ est top
*luh dee-jay ay top*

**do you come here often?**
tu viens souvent ici ?
*tU vyAN soo-vON ee-see ?*

**can I buy you a drink?**
je t'offre quelque chose à boire ?
*zhuh tofr kel-kuh-shohz a bwar ?*

**thanks, but I'm with my boyfriend**
merci, mais je suis avec mon copain
*mer-see, may zhuh swee avek mON koh-pAN*

**no thanks, I don't smoke**
non merci, je ne fume pas
*nON mer-see, zhuh nuh fUm pa*

## Understanding

| | |
|---|---|
| **avec conso** | first drink included |
| **gratuit pour les filles avant minuit** | ladies free up to midnight |
| **vestiaire** | cloakroom |

**il y a une soirée chez Magali**
there's a party at Magali's place

**tu veux danser ?**
do you want to dance?

**je t'offre quelque chose à boire ?**
can I buy you a drink?

**est-ce que tu aurais du feu ?**
have you got a light?

**est-ce que tu aurais une cigarette ?**
have you got a cigarette?

**est-ce qu'on peut se revoir ?**
can we see each other again?

**je te raccompagne ?**
can I see you home?

# TOURISM AND SIGHTSEEING

France has an impressive range of museums and art galleries. Opening hours vary, but most are open from about 10am to 7pm. Some of the larger ones stay open late on Wednesdays or Thursdays. Note that local museums are closed on Mondays and national ones on Tuesdays (except for the Musée d'Orsay in Paris, which is closed on Mondays).

The best thing to do is to visit the local tourist information centre (**office de tourisme**), which will have up-to-date information on opening hours and closing days for the museums and monuments you are interested in. You will also find a range of leaflets on local places of interest, castles that are open to the public, maps and so on.

## The basics

| | |
|---|---|
| ancient | ancien *ONs-yAN* |
| antique | antique *ON-teek* |
| area | quartier *kar-tyay* |
| castle | château *sha-toh* |
| cathedral | cathédrale *ka-tay-dral* |
| century | siècle *syekl* |
| church | église *ay-gleez* |
| exhibition | exposition *eks-poh-zees-yON* |
| famous | célèbre *say-lebr* |
| gallery | galerie *gal-ree* |
| modern art | art moderne *ar moh-dern* |
| mosque | mosquée *mos-kay* |
| museum | musée *mU-zay* |
| painting | tableau *ta-bloh* |
| park | parc *park* |
| ruins | ruines *rween* |
| sculpture | sculpture *skUl-tUr* |

| statue | statue *sta-tU* |
| street map | plan (de la ville) *plON (duh la veel)* |
| synagogue | synagogue *see-na-gog* |
| tour guide | guide *geed* |
| tourist | touriste *too-reest* |
| tourist information centre | office de tourisme *oh-fees duh too-reezm* |
| town centre | centre-ville *sON-truh veel* |

## Expressing yourself

**I'd like some information on …**
j'aimerais avoir des renseignements sur …
*zhay-muh-ray av-war day rON-sen-yuh-mON sUr …*

**can you tell me where the tourist information centre is?**
pourriez-vous m'indiquer où est l'office de tourisme ?
*poor-yay-voo mAN-dee-kay oo ay loh-fees duh too-reezm ?*

**do you have a street map of the town?**
est-ce que vous auriez un plan de la ville ?
*ess kuh vooz ohr-yay AN plON duh la veel ?*

**I was told there's an old abbey you can visit**
on m'a dit qu'il y a une vieille abbaye qu'on peut visiter
*ON ma dee keel ya Un vee-ey abay-ee kON puh vee-zee-tay*

**can you show me where it is on the map?**
pourriez-vous me montrer où c'est sur le plan ?
*poor-yay-voo muh mON-tray oo say sUr luh plON ?*

**how do you get there?**
comment on y va ?
*koh-mON ONn ee va ?*

**is it free?**
c'est gratuit ?
*say gra-twee ?*

**when was it built?**
ça date de quand ?
*sa dat duh kON ?*

## Understanding

| | |
|---|---|
| **en cours de rénovation** | renovation work in progress |
| **en cours de restauration** | restoration work in progress |
| **entrée libre** | admission free |
| **fermé** | closed |
| **ouvert** | open |
| **vieille ville** | old town |
| **visite guidée** | guided tour |
| **vous êtes ici** | you are here *(on a map)* |

**il faut vous renseigner sur place**
you'll have to ask when you get there

**la prochaine visite guidée commence à 14 heures**
the next guided tour starts at 2pm

# MUSEUMS, EXHIBITIONS AND MONUMENTS

## Expressing yourself

**I've heard there's a very good ... exhibition on at the moment**
il paraît qu'il y a une très bonne exposition sur ... en ce moment
*eel pa-ray keel ya Un tray bon eks-poh-zees-yON sUr ... ON suh moh-mON*

**how much is it to get in?**
combien coûte l'entrée ?
*kON-byAN koot lON-tray ?*

**is there a charge for admission?**
est-ce que l'entrée est payante ?
*ess kuh lON-tray ay pay-yONt ?*

**is this ticket valid for the exhibition as well?**
ce billet est-il valable aussi pour l'exposition (temporaire) ?
*suh bee-yay et-eel va-labl oh-see poor leks-poh-zees-yON (tON-poh-rer) ?*

**are there any discounts for young people?**
est-ce qu'il y a des réductions pour les jeunes ?
*ess keel ya day ray-dUks-yON poor lay zhuhn ?*

**is it open on Sundays?**
est-ce que c'est ouvert le dimanche ?
*ess kuh sayt oo-ver luh dee-mONsh ?*

**two concessions and one full price, please**
deux tarifs réduits et un plein tarif, s'il vous plaît
*duh ta-reef ray-dwee ay AN plAN ta-reef, seel voo play*

**I have a student card**
j'ai une carte d'étudiant
*zhay Un kart day-tU-dyON*

## Understanding

| | |
|---|---|
| **audiophone** | audioguide |
| **billeterie** | ticket office |
| **exposition temporaire** | temporary exhibition |
| **exposition permanente** | permanent exhibition |
| **flash interdit** | no flash photography |
| **ne pas toucher, merci** | please do not touch |
| **photos interdites** | no photography |
| **plein tarif** | full price |
| **sens de la visite** | this way |
| **silence, s'il vous plaît** | silence, please |
| **tarif réduit** | concession |

**l'entrée pour le musée coûte …**
admission to the museum costs …

**avec ce ticket, vous avez aussi accès à l'exposition**
this ticket also allows you access to the exhibition

**est-ce que vous avez une carte d'étudiant ?**
do you have your student card?

# GIVING YOUR IMPRESSIONS

## Expressing yourself

**it's beautiful**
c'est magnifique
*say ma-nee-feek*

**it was beautiful**
c'était magnifique
*say-tay ma-nee-feek*

**it's fantastic**
c'est formidable
*say for-mee-dabl*

**it was fantastic**
c'était formidable
*say-tay for-mee-dabl*

**I really enjoyed it**
j'ai beaucoup aimé
*zhay boh-koo ay-may*

**I didn't like it that much**
je n'ai pas tellement aimé
*zhuh nay pa tel-mON ay-may*

**it was a bit boring**
c'était un peu ennuyeux
*say-tay AN puh ON-nwee-yuh*

**it's very touristy**
c'est très touristique
*say tray too-rees-teek*

**I'm not really a fan of modern art**
je ne suis pas vraiment fan d'art moderne
*zhuh nuh swee pa vray-mON fan dar moh-dern*

**it's expensive for what it is**
c'est cher pour ce que c'est
*say sher poors kuh say*

**it was really crowded**
il y avait énormément de monde
*eel yavay ay-nor-may-mON duh mONd*

**we didn't go in the end, the queue was too long**
finalement on n'y est pas allés, il y avait trop de queue
*fee-nal-mON ON nee yay paz alay, eel yavay troh duh kuh*

**we didn't have time to see everything**
on n'a pas eu le temps de tout voir
*ON na paz U luh tON duh too vwar*

## Understanding

**vous devriez vraiment aller voir ...**
you really must go and see ...

**je vous recommande d'aller à ...**
I recommend going to ...

**il y a une vue superbe sur toute la ville**
there's a wonderful view over the whole city

**c'est devenu un peu trop touristique**
it's become a bit too touristy

**la côte a été complètement défigurée**
the coast has been completely ruined

# SPORTS AND GAMES

France has the largest skiing area in the world, with over 8,000 km of slopes, making it a paradise for all winter sports (**sports d'hiver**) fans. There are ski resorts (**stations de ski**) in all the mountainous areas, although the main resorts are in the Alps and the Pyrenees.

The Atlantic coast offers great waters for surfing, especially in the French Basque country and the Landes region, but surfers also brave the chillier waters of Brittany and Normandy.

France's beautiful and varied landscape is a paradise for walkers. There is an excellent system of hiking paths (**sentiers de randonnée**), which are clearly marked and signposted: **PR** for **petite randonnée** (short distance, colour-coded yellow and white) and **GR** for **grande randonnée** (long-distance, colour-coded red and white). Maps and guides of these are available in local tourist offices (**offices de tourisme**) and also in newsagents. Cycling is also popular and mountain bikes (**VTT, vélo tout terrain**) can be hired in most towns and larger villages.

Rugby and football are two other French passions, France being amongst the top teams in the world for each sport. And, of course, there is the typically French sport of **pétanque** (bowls), which you will see played in many towns and villages in the country.

## The basics

| | |
|---|---|
| ball | *(large)* **ballon** *ba-lON*, *(small)* **balle** *bal* |
| basketball | **basket** *ba-sket* |
| bike | **vélo** *vay-loh* |
| board game | **jeu de société** *zhuh duh soh-syay-tay* |
| cards | **cartes** *kart* |
| chess | **échecs** *ay-shek* |
| cross-country skiing | **ski de fond** *skee duh fON* |
| downhill skiing | **ski alpin** *skee alpAN* |
| football | **football** *foot-bol* |

| | |
|---|---|
| **hiking path** | sentier de randonnée *sON-tyay duh rON-doh-nay* |
| **match** | match *match* |
| **mountain biking** | VTT *vay-tay-tay* |
| **pool** (game) | billard (américain) *bee-yar (a-may-ree-kAN)* |
| **rugby** | rugby *rUg-bee* |
| **snowboarding** | snowboard *snoh-bord* |
| **sport** | sport *spor* |
| **surfing** | surf *suhrf* |
| **swimming** | natation *na-ta-syON* |
| **swimming pool** | piscine *pee-seen* |
| **table football** | baby-foot *ba-bee foot* |
| **tennis** | tennis *tay-nees* |
| **trip** | excursion *eks-kUr-syON* |
| **to go cycling** | faire du vélo *fer dU vay-loh* |
| **to go hiking** | faire de la randonnée *fer duh la rON-doh-nay* |
| **to have a game of ...** | faire une partie de ... *fer Un par-tee duh ...* |
| **to hire** | louer *loo-ay* |
| **to play** | jouer à *zhoo-ay a* |
| **to ski** | skier *skee-yay* |

## Expressing yourself

**are there ... lessons available?**
est-ce qu'il y a des cours de ... ?
*ess keel ya day koor duh ... ?*

**I'd like to hire ... for an hour**
je voudrais louer ... pour une heure
*zhuh voo-dray loo-ay ... poor Un uhr*

**how much is it per person per hour?**
c'est combien par heure et par personne ?
*say kON-byAN par uhr ay par per-son ?*

**I'm not very sporty**
je ne suis pas très sportif
*zhuh nuh swee pa tray spor-teef*

**I've never done it before**
je n'en ai jamais fait
*zhuh nONn ay zha-may fay*

**I've done it once or twice, a long time ago**
j'en ai fait une ou deux fois, il y a longtemps
*zhON ay fay Un oo duh fwa, eel ya lON-tON*

| | |
|---|---|
| **I'm exhausted!** | **we played ...** |
| je suis épuisé ! | on a joué à ... |
| *zhuh sweez ay-pwee-zay !* | *ON a zhoo-ay a ...* |

**I'd like to go and watch a football match**
j'aimerais aller voir un match de foot
*zhaym-ray alay vwar AN match duh foot*

**shall we stop for a picnic?**
on s'arrête pour pique-niquer ?
*ON sa-ret poor peek-nee-kay ?*

## Understanding

**location de ...**            ... for hire

**est-ce que vous avez des notions ou vous êtes complètement débutant ?**
do you have any experience, or are you a complete beginner?

**il faut verser une caution de ...**
there is a deposit of ...

**l'assurance est obligatoire et coûte ...**
insurance is compulsory and costs ...

# HIKING

### Expressing yourself

**are there any hiking paths around here?**
est-ce qu'il y a des sentiers de randonnée par ici ?
*ess keel ya day sON-tyay duh rON-doh-nay par ee-see ?*

**I'm looking for a guide to the hiking paths around here**
je cherche un guide des sentiers de randonnée de la région
*zhuh shersh AN geed day sON-tyay duh rON-doh-nay duh la rayzh-yON*

**I've heard there's a nice walk by the lake**
il paraît qu'il y a une belle balade au bord du lac
*eel pa-ray keel ya Un bel ba-lad oh bor dU lak*

**we're looking for a short walk somewhere round here**
on cherche une petite balade à faire dans le coin
*ON shersh Un puh-teet ba-lad a fer dON luh kwAN*

**how long does the hike take?**
combien dure la randonnée ?
*kON-byAN dUr la rON-doh-nay ?*

**is it very steep?**
ça monte beaucoup ?
*sa mONt boh-koo ?*

**where's the start of the path?**
où démarre le sentier ?
*oo day-mar luh sON-tyay ?*

**is the path waymarked?**
est-ce que le sentier est bien balisé ?
*ess kuh luh sON-tyay ay byAN ba-lee-zay ?*

**is it a circular path?**
est-ce que c'est un sentier en boucle ?
*ess kuh sayt AN sONt-yay ON bookl ?*

## Understanding

**durée moyenne**   average duration *(of walk)*

**c'est une randonnée d'environ trois heures sans compter les pauses**
it's about three hours' walk not including rest stops

**prévoyez un K-Way® et des chaussures de randonnée**
bring a waterproof jacket and walking shoes

# SKIING AND SNOWBOARDING

## Expressing yourself

**I'd like to hire skis, poles and boots**
je voudrais louer des skis, des bâtons et des chaussures de ski
*zhuh voo-dray loo-ay day skee, day ba-tON ay day shoh-sUr duh skee*

**I'd like to hire a snowboard**
je voudrais louer une planche de snowboard
*zhuh voo-dray loo-ay Un plONsh duh snoh-bord*

**they're too big/small**
elles sont trop grandes/petites
*el sON troh grONd/puh-teet*

**a day pass**
un forfait d'une journée
*AN for-fay dUn zhoor-nay*

**I'm a complete beginner**
je n'en ai jamais fait
*zhuh nONn ay zha-may fay*

| | |
|---|---|
| forfait | pass |
| remontée (mécanique) | ski lift |
| télésiège | chair lift |
| tire-fesses | T-bar, button lift |

# OTHER SPORTS

### Expressing yourself

**where can we hire bikes?**
où est-ce qu'on peut louer des vélos ?
*oo ess kON puh loo-ay day vay-loh ?*

**are there any cycle paths?**
est-ce qu'il y a des pistes cyclables ?
*ess keel ya day peestuh see-klabl ?*

**does anyone have a football?**
est-ce que quelqu'un aurait un ballon de foot ?
*ess kuh kel-kAN oh-ray AN ba-lON duh foot ?*

**which team do you support?** **I support ...**
vous êtes pour quelle équipe ? je suis pour ...
*vooz et poor kel ay-keep ?* *zhuh swee poor ...*

**is there an open-air swimming pool?**
est-ce qu'il y a une piscine en plein air ?
*ess keel ya Un pee-seen ON plen er ?*

**I've never been diving before**
je n'ai jamais fait de plongée
*zhuh nay zha-may fay duh plON-zhay*

SPORTS AND GAMES

77

**I'd like to take beginners' sailing lessons**
je voudrais prendre des cours de voile pour débutants
*zhuh voo-dray prONdr day koor duh vwal poor day-bU-tON*

**I run for half an hour every morning**
je cours tous les matins une demi-heure
*zhuh koor too lay ma-tAN Un duh-mee uhr*

**what do I do if the kayak capsizes?**
qu'est-ce que je fais si le kayak se renverse ?
*kess kuh zhuh fay see luh ka-yak suh rON-vers ?*

## Understanding

**il y a un court de tennis municipal près de la gare**
there's a public tennis court not far from the station

**le court de tennis est occupé**
the tennis court's occupied

**c'est la première fois que vous montez à cheval ?**
is this the first time you've been horse-riding?

**est-ce que vous savez nager ?**
can you swim?

**est-ce que tu joues au basket ?**
do you play basketball?

# INDOOR GAMES

### Expressing yourself

**it's your turn**
c'est ton tour
*say tON toor*

**shall we have a game of cards?**
on se fait une partie de cartes ?
*ON suh fay UN par-tee duh kart ?*

**does anyone know any good card games?**
est-ce que quelqu'un connaît un bon jeu de cartes ?
*ess kuh kel-kAN koh-nay AN bON zhuh duh kart ?*

**is anyone up for a game of Monopoly®?**
ça vous dit de jouer au Monopoly® ?
*sa voo dee duh zhoo-ay oh moh-noh-poh-lee ?*

## Understanding

**est-ce que tu sais jouer aux échecs ?**
do you know how to play chess?

**est-ce que tu as un jeu de cartes ?**
do you have a pack of cards?

---

### Some informal expressions

**je suis rétamé/crevé** I'm knackered
**il m'a écrasé** he thrashed me

---

# SHOPPING

Traditionally, most shops in France are closed on Mondays. This is still true of many smaller shops, including butchers and many bakers. However, superstores (**grandes surfaces**) and the bigger supermarkets (**supermarchés**) are open on Mondays. Superstores stay open all day and until at least 8pm and are usually closed on Sundays. The majority of other shops close between 12 and 2 and butchers, bakers, greengrocers etc are usually closed until 3pm. Small shops close at 7pm, though in big cities you may find tiny grocery shops that stay open until around 10pm. You can usually find a baker's open on Sunday mornings until midday and in some places other food shops.

Open-air markets (**marchés**) are a colourful institution and can be found all over the country. In big cities there will usually be a central daily market. Small towns and villages will have a weekly market and in big cities there are numerous local markets with different opening days. Markets are a morning event. Stalls close down between midday and 1pm.

Payment by card is accepted in almost all shops although smaller ones may impose a minimum spend. You may be asked to type in your PIN number and may possibly be asked for ID. Otherwise, you just sign the receipt as in Britain.

Note that you can only buy cigarettes in state-licensed tobacconists (**bureaux de tabac**). These have a red lozenge-shaped sign, usually illuminated. They close at 7pm but a number of cafés are also licensed tobacconists and carry the lozenge sign.

Alcohol can be bought in supermarkets, grocery shops and specialist wine stores, but there is no equivalent of British off-licences that stay open late in the evening.

If you are buying a present of any sort, it is absolutely standard to have it gift-wrapped free of charge.

### Some informal expressions

**c'est de l'arnaque** that's a rip-off
**je n'ai pas un rond** I'm skint
**ça coûte les yeux de la tête** it costs an arm and a leg

## The basics

| | |
|---|---|
| bakery | boulangerie *boo-lONzh-ree* |
| butcher's | boucherie *boosh-ree* |
| cash desk | caisse *kess* |
| cheap | pas cher *pa sher*, bon marché *bON mar-shay* |
| checkout | caisse *kess* |
| clothes | vêtements *vet-mON* |
| department store | grand magasin *grON ma-ga-zAN* |
| expensive | cher *sher* |
| gram | gramme *gram* |
| grocer's | épicerie *ay-pees-ree* |
| hypermarket | hypermarché *ee-per-mar-shay* |
| kilo | kilo *kee-loh* |
| present | cadeau *ka-doh* |
| price | prix *pree* |
| receipt | ticket de caisse *tee-kay duh kess* |
| sales | soldes *sold* |
| sales assistant | *(male)* vendeur *vON-duhr*, *(female)* vendeuse *vON-duhz* |
| shop | magasin *ma-ga-zAN* |
| shopping centre | centre commercial *sONtr koh-mers-yal* |
| souvenir | souvenir *soov-neer* |
| supermarket | supermarché *sUper-mar-shay* |
| to buy | acheter *ash-tay* |
| to cost | coûter *koo-tay* |
| to pay | payer *pay-yay* |
| to refund | rembourser *rON-boor-say* |
| to sell | vendre *vONdr* |

## Expressing yourself

**is there a supermarket near here?**
est-ce qu'il y a un supermarché par ici ?
*ess keel ya AN sUper-mar-shay par ee-see ?*

**where can I buy cigarettes?**
où est-ce que je peux acheter des cigarettes ?
*oo ess kuh zhuh puh ash-tay day see-ga-ret ?*

**I'd like ...**
je voudrais ...
*zhuh voo-dray ...*

**I'm looking for ...**
je cherche ...
*zhuh shersh ...*

**do you sell ...?**
est-ce que vous avez ... ?
*ess kuh vooz avay ... ?*

**do you know where I might find ...?**
savez-vous où je pourrais trouver ... ?
*sa-vay-voo oo zhuh poo-ray troo-vay ... ?*

**can you order it for me?**
est-ce que vous pouvez me le/la commander ?
*ess kuh voo poo-vay muh luh/la koh-mON-day ?*

**how much is this?**
ça coûte combien ?
*sa koot kON-byAN ?*

**I'll take it**
je le/la prends
*zhuh luh/la prON*

**I haven't got much money**
je n'ai pas beaucoup d'argent
*zhuh nay pa boh-koo dar-zhON*

**I haven't got enough money**
je n'ai pas assez d'argent
*zhuh nay paz a-say dar-zhON*

**that's everything, thanks**
ça sera tout, merci
*sa suh-ra too, mer-see*

**can I have a (plastic) bag?**
est-ce que je peux avoir un sac plastique ?
*ess kuh zhuh puh av-war AN sak plas-teek ?*

**I think you've made a mistake with my change**
je crois que vous avez fait une erreur en me rendant la monnaie
*zhuh krwa kuh vooz avay fay Un ay-ruhr ON muh rON-dON la moh-nay*

## Understanding

| | |
|---|---|
| **fermé** | closed |
| **horaires (d'ouverture)** | opening hours |
| **nocturne le jeudi** | late-night opening Thursdays |
| **offre spéciale** | special offer |
| **ouvert** | open |
| **promotion** | special offer |
| **soldes** | sales |

**et avec ceci ?**
will there be anything else?

# PAYING

## Expressing yourself

**where do I pay?**
où est-ce qu'on paye ?
*oo ess kON pey ?*

**how much do I owe you?**
combien je vous dois ?
*kON-byAN zh-voo dwa ?*

**could you write it down for me, please?**
est-ce que vous pourriez me l'écrire, s'il vous plaît ?
*ess kuh voo poor-yay muh lay-kreer, seel voo play ?*

**I'll pay in cash**
je vais payer en liquide
*zhuh vay pay-yay ON lee-keed*

**can I pay by credit card?**
est-ce que je peux payer par carte ?
*ess kuh zhuh puh pay-yay par kart ?*

**I'm sorry, I haven't got any change**
je suis désolé, je n'ai pas du tout de monnaie
*zhuh swee day-zoh-lay, zhuh nay pa dU too duh moh-nay*

**can I have a receipt?**
est-ce que je peux avoir le ticket de caisse ?
*ess kuh zhuh puh av-war luh tee-kay duh kess ?*

## Understanding

**payez en caisse**
pay at the cash desk

**vous réglez comment ?**
how would you like to pay?

**vous n'avez pas plus petit ?**
do you have anything smaller?

**je vais vous demander une pièce d'identité, s'il vous plaît**
have you got any ID?

**je vais vous demander une signature ici, s'il vous plaît**
could you sign here, please?

# FOOD

### Expressing yourself

**where can I buy food around here?**
où est-ce que je peux acheter à manger par ici ?
*oo ess kuh zhuh puh ash-tay a mON-zhay par ee-see ?*

**is there a market?**
est-ce qu'il y a un marché ?
*ess keel ya AN mar-shay ?*

**is there a bakery around here?**
est-ce qu'il y a une boulangerie par ici ?
*ess keel ya Un boo-lONzh-ree par ee-see ?*

**I'm looking for the cereal aisle**
je cherche le rayon des céréales
*zhuh shersh luh ray-yON day say-ray-al*

**I'd like five slices of ham**
je voudrais cinq tranches de jambon
*zhuh voo-dray sANk trONsh duh zhON-bON*

**I'd like some of that goat's cheese**
je voudrais un peu de ce fromage de chèvre
*zhuh voo-dray AN puh duh suh froh-mazh duh shevr*

**it's for four people**
c'est pour quatre personnes
*say poor kat per-son*

**about 300 grams**
environ 300 grammes
*ON-vee-rON trwa sON gram*

**a kilo of apples, please**
un kilo de pommes, s'il vous plaît
*AN kee-loh duh pom, seel voo play*

**a bit less**
un peu moins
*AN puh mwAN*

**a bit more**
un peu plus
*AN puh plUs*

**can I taste it?**
est-ce qu'il serait possible de goûter ?
*ess keel suh-ray poh-seebl duh goo-tay ?*

**does it travel well?**
est-ce que ça peut voyager ?
*ess kuh sa puh vwa-ya-zhay ?*

## Understanding

**à consommer (de préférence) avant …**
best before …

**biologique**
organic

**maison**
homemade

**spécialités du pays**
local specialities

**il y a un marché tous les jours jusqu'à midi**
there's a market every day until midday

**il y a un épicier juste à côté qui reste ouvert tard le soir**
there's a grocer's just round the corner that's open late

# CLOTHES

### Expressing yourself

**I'm looking for the menswear section**
je cherche le rayon hommes
*zhuh shersh luh ray-yon om*

**can I try it on?**
est-ce que je peux l'essayer ?
*ess kuh zhuh puh lay-say-yay ?*

**no thanks, I'm just looking**
non, merci, je regarde seulement
*nON, mer-see, zhuh ruh-gard suhl-mON*

**I'd like to try the one in the window**
je voudrais essayer celui/celle qui est en vitrine
*zhuh voo-dray ay-say-yay suh-lwee/sel kee ay ON vee-treen*

SHOPPING

85

**I take a size 39** *(in shoes)*
je fais du 39
*zhuh fay dU trONt-nuhf*

**where are the changing rooms?**
où sont les cabines d'essayage ?
*oo sON lay ka-been day-say-yazh ?*

**it isn't quite right**
ça ne me va pas
*sa nuh muh va pa*

**it's too big/small**
c'est trop grand/petit
*say troh grON/puh-tee*

**do you have it in another colour?**
est-ce que vous l'avez dans une autre couleur ?
*ess kuh voo lavay dONz Un ohtr koo-luhr ?*

**do you have it in a smaller/bigger size?**
est-ce que vous l'avez dans une plus petite/grande taille ?
*ess kuh voo lavay dONz Un plU puh-teet/grONd ta-ee ?*

**do you have it in red?**
est-ce que vous l'avez en rouge ?
*ess kuh voo lavay ON roozh ?*

**yes, that's fine, I'll take it**
oui, c'est bon, je le/la prends
*wee, say bON, zhuh luh/la prON*

**no, I don't like it**
non, je n'aime pas
*nON, zhuh nem pa*

**I'll think about it**
je vais réfléchir
*zhuh vay ray-flay-sheer*

**I'd like to return this, it doesn't fit**
je voudrais rendre ceci, ça ne va pas
*zhuh voo-dray rONdr suh-see, sa nuh va pa*

**this ... has a hole in it, can I get a refund?**
ce/cette ... a un trou, est-ce que je pourrais me faire rembourser ?
*suh/set ... a AN troo, ess kuh zhuh poo-ray muh fer rON-boor-say ?*

## Understanding

| | |
|---|---|
| **cabines d'essayage** | changing rooms |
| **vêtements pour enfants** | children's clothes |
| **vêtements pour femmes** | ladieswear |
| **vêtements pour hommes** | menswear |

**les articles en solde ne sont ni repris ni échangés**
sale items cannot be returned or exchanged

**bonjour, je peux vous aider ?**
hello, can I help you?

**nous ne l'avons qu'en bleu et en noir**
we only have it in blue or black

**il ne nous en reste plus dans cette taille**
we don't have any left in that size

**ça vous va bien**
it suits you

**c'est bien votre taille**
it fits you really well

**vous pouvez le/la rendre si ça ne va pas**
you can bring it back if it doesn't fit

# SOUVENIRS AND PRESENTS

### Expressing yourself

**I'm looking for a present to take home**
je cherche un cadeau à ramener
*zhuh shersh AN ka-doh a ram-nay*

**I'd like something that's easy to transport**
je voudrais quelque chose de facile à transporter
*zhuh voo-dray kel kuh shohz duh fa-seel a trONs-por-tay*

**it's for a little girl of four**
c'est pour une petite fille de quatre ans
*say poor Un puh-teet fee duh katr ON*

**could you gift-wrap it for me?**
est-ce que vous pouvez me faire un paquet-cadeau ?
*ess kuh voo poo-vay muh fer AN pa-kay ka-doh ?*

### Understanding

**artisanal**
**fait main**

traditionally made
handmade

**combien êtes-vous prêt à dépenser ?**
how much do you want to spend?

**c'est pour offrir ?**
is it for a present?

**c'est typique de la région**
it's typical of the region

# PHOTOS

## The basics

| | |
|---|---|
| **black and white** | (en) noir et blanc *(ON) nwar ay blON* |
| **camera** | appareil photo *a-pa-rey foto* |
| **colour** | (en) couleur *(ON) koo-luhr* |
| **copy** | exemplaire *eg-zON-pler*, retirage *ruh-tee-razh* |
| **digital camera** | appareil photo numérique *a-pa-rey foto nU-may-reek* |
| **disposable camera** | appareil photo jetable *a-pa-rey foto zhuh-tabl* |
| **exposure** | pose *pohz* |
| **film** | pellicule *pay-lee-kUl* |
| **flash** | flash *flash* |
| **glossy** | brillant *bree-yON* |
| **matt** | mat *mat* |
| **memory card** | carte mémoire *kart may-mwar* |
| **negative** | négatif *nay-ga-teef* |
| **passport photo** | photo d'identité *foto dee-dON-tee-tay* |
| **photo** | photo *foto* |
| **photo booth** | Photomaton® *foto-ma-tON* |
| **reprint** | retirage *ruh-tee-razh* |
| **slide** | diapositive *dya-poh-zee-teev* |
| **to get photos developed** | faire développer des photos *fer day-vlo-pay day foto* |
| **to take a photo/ photos** | prendre une photo/des photos *prONdr Un foto/day foto* |

## Expressing yourself

**could you take a photo of us, please?**
est-ce que vous pourriez nous prendre une photo ?
*ess-kuh voo poor-yay noo prONdr Un foto ?*

**you just have to press this button**
il suffit d'appuyer sur ce bouton
*eel sU-fee da-pwee-yay sUr suh boo-tON*

**I'd like a 200 ASA colour film**
je voudrais une pellicule couleur 200 ASA
*zhuh voo-dray Un pay-lee-kUI koo-luhr duh sON aza*

**do you have black and white films?**
est-ce que vous avez des pellicules noir et blanc ?
*ess-kuh vooz avay day pay-lee-kUI nwar ay blON ?*

**how much is it to develop a film of 36 photos?**
combien coûte le développement d'une pellicule de 36 poses ?
*kON-byAN koot luh day-vlop-mON dUn pay-lee-kUI duh trONt see pohz ?*

**I'd like to have this film developed**
je voudrais faire développer cette pellicule
*zhuh voo-dray fer day-vlo-pay set pay-lee-kUI*

**I'd like extra copies of some of the photos**
je voudrais faire retirer certaines photos
*zhuh voo-dray fer ruh-tee-ray ser-ten foto*

**three copies of this one and two of this one**
trois exemplaires de cette photo et deux de celle-ci
*trwaz eg-zON-pler duh set foto ay duh duh sel-see*

**can I print my digital photos here?**
est-ce que vous développez les photos numériques ?
*ess-kuh voo day-vlo-pay lay foto nU-may-reek ?*

**can you put these photos on a CD for me?**
est-ce que vous pourriez mettre ces photos sur CD ?
*ess-kuh voo poor-yay metr say foto sUr say-day ?*

**do you sell memory cards?**
est-ce que vous avez des cartes mémoire ?
*ess-kuh vooz avay day kart may-mwar ?*

**I've come to pick up my photos**
je viens chercher mes photos
*zhuh vyAN sher-shay may foto*

**I've got a problem with my camera**
j'ai un problème avec mon appareil photo
*zhay AN proh-blem avek mON a-pa-rey foto*

**I don't know what it is**
je ne sais pas ce que c'est
*zhuh nuh say pass kuh say*

**the flash doesn't work**
le flash ne marche pas
*luh flash nuh marsh pa*

## Understanding

| | |
|---|---|
| **développement en 1 heure** | photos developed in one hour |
| **format standard** | standard format |
| **photos sur CD** | photos on CD |
| **service express** | express service |

**c'est peut-être la pile qui est morte**
maybe the battery's dead

**nous développons les photos numériques**
we can print digital photos

**c'est à quel nom ?**
what's the name, please?

**vous les voulez pour quand ?**
when do you want them for?

**on peut vous les développer en une heure**
we can develop them in an hour

**vos photos seront prêtes jeudi à partir de midi**
your photos will be ready on Thursday at midday

Banks in the Paris area are usually open from 10am to 5pm, Monday to Friday. In the rest of the country, they are open from Tuesday to Saturday and usually close for lunch between midday and 2pm. Some branches are open all day on Saturdays, some only in the morning. Many close early on the eve of a bank holiday. There are plenty of cashpoints (**distributeurs**) which take international cards, though your bank may charge you for withdrawals.

Not that French uses a comma rather than a dot for decimal points and that the euro symbol goes after the sum, so ten euros and fifteen cents is written 10,15€.

Some banks provide a currency exchange facility (**bureau de change**).

---

**Some informal expressions**
**fric, thune** cash
**tirer du fric** to get out some cash

---

### The basics

| | |
|---|---|
| **bank** | banque *bONk* |
| **bank account** | compte (bancaire) *kONt (bON-ker)* |
| **banknote** | billet *bee-yay* |
| **bureau de change** | bureau de change *bU-roh duh shONzh* |
| **cashpoint** | distributeur (automatique) *dees-tree-bU-tuhr (oh-toh-ma-teek)* |
| **change** | monnaie *moh-nay* |
| **coin** | pièce (de monnaie) *pee-yes (duh moh-nay)* |
| **commission** | commission *koh-mees-yON* |
| **credit card** | carte de crédit *kart duh kray-dee* |
| **euro** | euro *uh-roh* |
| **(euro) cent** | centime (d'euro) *sON-teem (duh-roh)* |

| **PIN (number)** | code confidentiel *kod kON-fee-dONs-yel* |
| **pound** *(currency)* | livre (sterling) *leev-ruh (ster-leeng)* |
| **transfer** | virement *veer-mON* |
| **Travellers Cheque®** | traveller's cheque® *trav-luhrz shek*, chèque de voyage *shek duh vwa-yazh* |
| **withdrawal** | retrait *ruh-tre* |
| **to change** | changer *shON-zhay* |
| **to withdraw** | retirer *ruh-tee-ray* |

## Expressing yourself

**where I can get some money changed?**
où est-ce que je peux changer de l'argent ?
*oo ess-kuh zhuh puh shON-zhay duh lar-zhON ?*

**are banks open on Saturdays?**
les banques sont-elles ouvertes le samedi ?
*lay bONk sONt-el oo-vert luh sam-dee ?*

**I'm looking for a cashpoint**
je cherche un distributeur
*zhuh shersh AN dees-tree-bU-tuhr*

**I'd like to change £100**
je voudrais changer 100 livres (sterling)
*zhuh voo-dray shON-zhay sON leev-ruh (ster-leeng)*

**what commission do you charge?**
qu'est que vous prenez comme commission ?
*kess-kuh voo pruh-nay kom koh-mees-yON ?*

**I'd like to transfer some money**
je voudrais faire un virement
*zhuh voo-dray fer AN veer-mON*

**the cashpoint has swallowed my card**
le distributeur a avalé ma carte
*luh dees-tree-bU-tuhr a ava-lay ma kart*

## Understanding

**composez votre code confidentiel puis validez**
please enter your PIN number and press enter

**autre montant**
other amount

**souhaitez-vous un ticket ?**
would you like a receipt?

**pour obtenir vos billets veuillez reprendre votre carte**
please remove your card and wait for your cash

**hors service**
out of service

# POST OFFICES

Postboxes in France are yellow and collection times are displayed on the box. Outside the post office (**bureau de poste**) there are usually two boxes, one for local mail with the name of the city or area and one for all other destinations (**autres destinations**). Stamps can be bought in post offices and tobacconists (**bureau de tabac**). The price for a stamp for the UK and other European countries is the same as for France. For other destinations, you should go to a post office. Most post offices are open Monday to Friday from 9am to 5pm. In small towns they close between midday and 2pm. They are open from 9am to midday on Saturdays.

## The basics

| | |
|---|---|
| airmail | par avion *par av-yON* |
| envelope | enveloppe *ONv-lop* |
| letter | lettre *letr* |
| mail | courrier *koor-yay* |
| parcel | colis *koh-lee*, paquet *pa-kay* |
| post | poste *post* |
| postbox | boîte aux lettres *bwat oh letr* |
| postcard | carte postale *kart pohs-tal* |
| postcode | code postal *kod pohs-tal* |
| post office | (bureau de) poste *(bU-roh duh) post* |
| stamp | timbre *tANbr* |
| to post | poster *pos-tay* |
| to send | envoyer *ON-vwa-yay* |
| to write | écrire *ay-kreer* |

## Expressing yourself

**is there a post office around here?**
est-ce qu'il y a un bureau de poste par ici ?
*es keel ya AN bU-roh duh post par ee-see ?*

**is there a postbox near here?**
est-ce qu'il y a une boîte aux lettres près d'ici ?
*ess keel ya Un bwat oh letr pray dee-see ?*

**what time does the post office close?**
à quelle heure ferme la poste ?
*a kel uhr ferm la post ?*

**do you sell stamps?**
est-ce que vous vendez des timbres ?
*ess kuh voo vON-day day tANbr ?*

**I'd like … stamps for the UK, please**
je voudrais … timbres pour le Royaume-Uni, s'il vous plaît
*zhuh voo-dray … tANbr poor luh rwa-yohm-Unee, seel voo play*

**I want to send this package by registered mail**
je veux envoyer ce colis en recommandé
*zhuh vuh ON-vwa-yay suh koh-lee ON ruh-koh-mON-day*

**how long will it take to arrive?**
ça va mettre combien de temps pour arriver ?
*sa va metr kON-byAN duh tON poor a-ree-vay ?*

**where can I buy envelopes?**
où est-ce que je peux acheter des enveloppes ?
*oo ess kuh zhuh puh ash-tay dayz ONv-lop ?*

**is there any post for me?**
est-ce qu'il y a du courrier pour moi ?
*ess keel ya dU koor-yay poor mwa ?*

POST OFFICES

## Understanding

| | |
|---|---|
| **dernière levée** | last collection |
| **destinataire** | addressee, recipient |
| **expéditeur** | sender |
| **première levée** | first collection |
| **recommandé** | registered |

**ça met entre 3 et 5 jours**
it'll take between three and five days

In France envelopes are addressed in much the same way as in the UK. However, if you are writing to someone in France, you should note that the postcode *precedes* the name of the town. The first two figures of the five-figure postcode indicate the department (**département**), ie the administrative area (07 in the address below is the code for the département Ardèche so it is not necessary to write "Ardèche" in the address). Here is a typical address:

Mme Céline Constantin
23 rue des Acacias
07440 Lamastre
France

The sender's address should be written on the back of the envelope at the top. Note that letters addressed to a country outside France must have the country name written in French. So, for the UK, **Royaume-Uni**.

The following abbreviations are commonly used in addresses:

**Av** (= **avenue**) avenue
**Bd** (= **boulevard**) boulevard
**B.P.** (= **boîte postale**) PO box
**Dest.** (= **destinataire**) addressee, recipient
**Exp.** (= **expéditeur**) sender
**Pl** (= **place**) square
**r.** (= **rue**) street
**rte** (= **route**) road

# INTERNET CAFÉS AND E-MAIL

**www**

The number of internet cafés (**cafés Internet**) in France is increasing rapidly. Internet use is widespread, and it is common practice to swap e-mail addresses with people. Note that the French use an AZERTY keyboard, the layout of which differs from the QWERTY one you will be familiar with.

An "at" sign is called **une arobase**, a dot is **un point** and a hyphen is **un tiret**. If part of the address is written as all one word, you say **en un seul mot**. For example, jeandelhourme@wanadoo.fr would read as "**jean delhourme (en un seul mot) arobase wanadoo point F R**".

## The basics

| | |
|---|---|
| **at sign** | arobase *a-roh-baz* |
| **e-mail** | e-mail *ee-meyl* |
| **e-mail address** | adresse e-mail *a-dres ee-meyl* |
| **Internet café** | café Internet *ka-fay AN-ter-net* |
| **key** | touche *toosh* |
| **keyboard** | clavier *kla-vyay* |
| **password** | mot de passe *moh duh pas* |
| **to copy** | copier *koh-pyay* |
| **to cut** | couper *koo-pay* |
| **to delete** | supprimer *sU-pree-may* |
| **to download** | télécharger *tay-lay-shar-zhay* |
| **to e-mail somebody** | envoyer un e-mail à quelqu'un *ON-vwa-yay AN nee-meyl a kel-kAN* |
| **to paste** | coller *koh-lay* |
| **to receive** | recevoir *ruh-suh-vwar* |
| **to save** | sauvegarder *sohv-gar-day* |
| **to send** | envoyer *ON-vwa-yay* |

## Expressing yourself

**is there an Internet café near here?**
est-ce qu'il y a un café Internet près d'ici ?
*ess keel ya AN ka-fay AN-ter-net pray dee-see ?*

**do you have an e-mail address?**
est-ce que vous avez une adresse e-mail ?
*ess kuh vooz avay Un a-dres ee-meyl ?*

**how do I get online?**
qu'est-ce que je dois faire pour me connecter ?
*kess kuh zhuh dwa fer poor muh koh-nek-tay ?*

**I'd just like to check my e-mails**
je voudrais juste consulter mes e-mails
*zhuh voo-dray jUst kON-sUl-tay mayz ee-meyl*

**would you mind helping me, I'm not sure what to do**
est-ce que vous pourriez m'aider, je ne sais pas vraiment ce qu'il faut
faire
*ess kuh voo poor-yay may-day, zhuh nuh say pa vray-mON suh keel foh fer*

**I can't find the at sign on this keyboard**
je ne trouve pas l'arobase sur ce clavier
*zhuh nuh troov pa la-roh-baz sUr suh kla-vyay*

**it's not working**
ça ne marche pas
*sa nuh marsh pa*

**there's something wrong with the computer, it's frozen**
il y a quelque chose qui ne va pas, l'ordinateur est bloqué
*eel ya kel-kuh shohz kee nuh va pa, lor-dee-na-tuhr ay bloh-kay*

**how much will it be for half an hour?**
ça coûte combien pour une demi-heure ?
*sa koot kON-byAN poor Un duh-mee-uhr ?*

**when do I pay?**
quand est-ce que je dois payer ?
*kONt ess kuh zhuh dwa pay-yay ?*

## Understanding

**boîte d'envoi**      outbox
**boîte de réception**    inbox

**il y a environ 20 minutes d'attente**
you'll have to wait for 20 minutes or so

**n'hésitez pas à demander si vous ne savez pas ce qu'il faut faire**
just ask if you're not sure what to do

**il vous suffit de taper votre mot de passe pour vous connecter**
just enter this password to log on

INTERNET CAFÉS, E-MAIL

ⓘ

Public telephones have their own numbers, as in the UK, so you can receive as well as make calls there. All phoneboxes take phonecards (**Télécartes®**) and most now accept credit cards. Phoneboxes that take coins (**pièces**) are now extremely rare.

Phonecards are sold in tobacconists (**bureaux de tabac**), post offices (**bureaux de poste**), souvenir shops and other retail outlets. You can also buy prepaid cards (**cartes prépayées**).

Phone numbers in France have 10 digits and always start with a 0. Note that the way of giving a French telephone number is to use double figures, so, for the number 04.75.06.30.51, a person will say: zéro quatre, soixante-quinze, zéro six, trente, cinquante et un.

The France Telecom number for directory enquiries is **12**. Note that if you are using a British mobile phone to call someone in France, you need to add the country code from Britain (0033), then omit the zero from the beginning of the French number. When phoning Britain, you don't need any international code.

To call the UK from a French landline, dial 00 44 followed by the full phone number, minus the first zero of the area code. To dial France from the UK, dial 00 33 and drop the first zero of the phone number.

## The basics

| | |
|---|---|
| answering machine | répondeur *ray-pON-duhr* |
| call | appel *a-pel* |
| directory enquiries | renseignements *rON-sen-yuh-mON* |
| hello | allô *a-loh* |
| international call | appel international *a-pel AN-ter-nas-yoh-nal* |
| local call | appel local *a-pel loh-kal* |
| message | message *may-sazh* |
| mobile | portable *por-tabl* |

| | |
|---|---|
| national call | appel national *a-pel nas-yoh-nal* |
| phone | téléphone *tay-lay-fon* |
| phone book | annuaire *a-nU-er* |
| phone box | cabine téléphonique *ka-been tay-lay-fo-neek* |
| phone call | appel *a-pel* |
| phonecard | carte de téléphone *kart duh tay-lay-fon*, Télécarte® *tay-lay-kart* |
| phone number | numéro de téléphone *nU-may-roh duh tay-lay-fon* |
| ringtone | sonnerie *so-ne-ree* |
| text message | SMS *es-em-es* |
| Yellow Pages® | Pages Jaunes® *pazh zhohn* |
| to call somebody | appeler quelqu'un *a-play kel-kAN* |
| to phone somebody | téléphoner à quelqu'un *tay-lay-fo-nay a kel-kAN* |
| to recharge | recharger *ruh-shar-zhay* |
| to text somebody | envoyer un SMS à quelqu'un *ON-vwa-yay UN es-em-es a kel-kAN* |

## Expressing yourself

**where can I buy a phonecard?**
où est-ce que je peux acheter une carte de téléphone ?
*oo ess kuh zhuh puh ash-tay Un kart duh tay-lay-fon ?*

**I'd like to make a reverse-charge call**
je voudrais appeler en PCV
*zhuh voo-dray a-play ON pay-say-vay*

**is there a phone box near here, please?**
excusez-moi, est-ce qu'il y a une cabine téléphonique près d'ici ?
*eks-kU-zay-mwa, ess keel ya Un ka-been tay-lay-fo-neek pray dee-see ?*

**can I plug my phone in here to recharge it?**
est-ce que je peux brancher mon portable ici pour le recharger ?
*ess kuh zhuh puh brON-shay mON por-tabl ee-see poor luh ruh-shar-zhay ?*

**do you have a mobile number?**
est-ce que vous avez un numéro de portable ?
*ess kuh vooz a-vay AN nU-may-roh duh por-tabl ?*

**where can I contact you?**
où est-ce que je peux vous joindre ?
*oo ess kuh zhuh puh voo zhwANdr ?*

**did you get my message?**
avez-vous eu mon message ?
*a-vay voo U mON may-sazh ?*

## Understanding

**le numéro que vous avez demandé n'est pas attribué**
the number you have dialled has not been recognized

**appuyez sur la touche dièse/étoile**
please press the hash/star key

# MAKING A CALL

### Expressing yourself

**hello, this is David Brown (speaking)**
allô, bonjour, David Brown à l'appareil
*a-loh, bON-zhoor, David Brown a la-pa-rey*

**hello, could I speak to..., please?**
allô, bonjour, est-ce que je pourrais parler à ... ?
*a-loh, bON-zhoor, ess kuh zhuh poo-ray par-lay a ... ?*

**hello, is that Caroline?**
allô, Caroline ?
*a-loh, ka-roh-leen ?*

**do you speak English?**
est-ce que vous parlez anglais ?
*ess kuh voo par-lay ON-glay ?*

**could you speak more slowly, please?**
est-ce que vous pourriez parler plus lentement, s'il vous plaît ?
*ess kuh voo poor-yay par-lay plU lON-tuh-mON, seel voo play ?*

**I can't hear you, could you speak up, please?**
je ne vous entends pas bien, est-ce que vous pourriez parler plus fort ?
*zhuh nuh vooz ON-tON pa byAN, ess kuh voo poor-yay par-lay plU for ?*

TELEPHONE

**could you tell him/her I called?**
est-ce que vous pourriez lui dire que j'ai appelé ?
*ess kuh voo poor-yay lwee deer kuh zhay a-play ?*

**could you ask him/her to call me back?**
est-ce que vous pourriez lui dire de me rappeler ?
*ess kuh voo poor-yay lwee deer duh muh ra-play ?*

**I'll call back later**
je rappellerai plus tard
*zhuh ra-pel-ray plU tar*

**thank you, goodbye**
merci, au revoir
*mer-see, oh ruh-vwar*

**my name is … and my number is …**
je suis … et mon numéro est le …
*zhuh swee … ay mON nU-may-roh ay luh …*

**do you know when he/she might be available?**
est-ce que vous savez quand je pourrai le/la joindre ?
*ess kuh voo sa-vay kON zhuh poo-ray luh/la zhwANdr ?*

## Understanding

**qui est à l'appareil ?**
who's calling?

**un instant, s'il vous plaît**
hold on

**vous vous êtes trompé de numéro**
you've got the wrong number

**il/elle n'est pas là pour le moment**
he's/she's not here at the moment

**est-ce que vous voulez laisser un message ?**
do you want to leave a message?

**je lui dirai que vous avez appelé**
I'll tell him/her you called

**je lui dirai de vous rappeler**
I'll ask him/her to call you back

**je vous le/la passe**
I'll just hand you over to him/her

# PROBLEMS

## Expressing yourself

**I don't know the code**
je ne connais pas l'indicatif
*zhuh nuh ko-nay pa lAN-dee-ka-teef*

**it's engaged**
ça sonne occupé
*sa son oh-kU-pay*

**there's no reply**
il n'y a personne
*eel nya per-son*

**I couldn't get through**
je n'ai pas réussi à le/la joindre
*zhuh nay pa ray-U-see a luh/la zhwANdr*

**I don't have much credit left on my phone**
il ne me reste plus beaucoup de crédit sur mon portable
*eel nuh muh rest plU boh-koo duh kray-dee sUr mON por-tabl*

**we're about to get cut off**
ça va couper
*sa va koo-pay*

**the reception's really bad**
il y a une très mauvaise réception
*eel ya Un tray moh-vez ray-seps-yON*

**I can't get a signal**
il n'y a pas de réception
*eel nya pa duh ray-seps-yON*

---

### Some informal expressions

**passer un coup de fil à quelqu'un** to give somebody a ring
**elle m'a raccroché au nez** she hung up on me

---

If you are an EU national, pick up an E111 form from the Post Office before you go to France. This ensures that the cost of any medical treatment you may need in France will be refunded to you when you return home, on production of a receipt.

You can visit a health centre (**centre médical**) or a medical practice (**cabinet médical**). Also, in serious cases, you can go to a hospital casualty department (**urgences**). Doctors can be either **conventionné** (working for the national health service and charging set rates) or private. The phone number for the emergency medical services (**SAMU**) is 15. You can find a list of general practitioners in the Yellow Pages® of the telephone directory (**annuaire**) for your area. Look up the heading **Médecins** then **Médecine générale**, then the town or village where you are. On Sundays and after hours, the name and telephone number of the duty doctor (**médecin de garde**) is posted outside surgeries. In the Yellow Pages®, specialists and practitioners of alternative medicine are listed after general practitioners, in order of specialization.

Medicines can only be bought from a chemist's (**pharmacie**). This includes over the counter medicines like aspirin and paracetamol. Chemists are open from 9am to 7 or 8pm from Monday to Saturday, though many close between midday and 2pm. After hours there is always a duty pharmacy (**pharmacie de garde**) open in the area.

## The basics

| | |
|---|---|
| allergy | allergie *a-ler-zhee* |
| ambulance | ambulance *ON-bU-lONs* |
| aspirin | aspirine *as-pee-reen* |
| blood | sang *sON* |
| broken | cassé *ka-say* |
| casualty (department) | urgences *Ur-zhONs* |
| chemist's | pharmacie *far-ma-see* |
| condom | préservatif *pray-zer-va-teef* |

| dentist | dentiste *dON-teest* |
| diarrhoea | diarrhée *dya-ray* |
| doctor | médecin *mayd-sAN* |
| food poisoning | intoxication alimentaire *AN-tok-see-kas-yON a-lee-mON-ter* |
| GP | (médecin) généraliste *(mayd-sAN) zhay-nay-ra-leest* |
| gynaecologist | gynécologue *zhee-nay-koh-log* |
| hospital | hôpital *oh-pee-tal* |
| infection | infection *AN-feks-yON* |
| medicine | médicament *may-dee-ka-mON* |
| optician | opticien *op-tees-yAN* |
| painkiller | calmant *kal-mON* |
| period(s) | règles *regl* |
| plaster | pansement *pONs-mON* |
| prescription | ordonnance *or-doh-nONs* |
| rash | éruption cutanée *ay-rUps-yON kU-ta-nay* |
| spot | bouton *boo-tON* |
| sunburn | coup de soleil *koo duh soh-ley* |
| surgical spirit | alcool à 90°C *al-kol a kat-ruh vAN dees* |
| tablet | comprimé *kON-pree-may* |
| temperature | fièvre *fee-yevr* |
| vaccination | vaccin *vak-sAN* |
| x-ray | radio *ra-dyoh* |
| to disinfect | désinfecter *day-zAN-fek-tay* |
| to faint | s'évanouir *say-va-nweer* |
| to vomit | vomir *voh-meer* |

## Expressing yourself

**does anyone have an aspirin/a tampon/a plaster, by any chance?**
est-ce que quelqu'un aurait une aspirine/un tampon/un pansement par hasard ?
*ess kuh kel-kAN oh-ray UN as-pee-reen/AN tON-pON/AN pONs-mON par a-zar ?*

**I need to see a doctor**
il faut que j'aille voir un médecin
*eel foh kuh zha-ee vwar AN mayd-sAN*

**where can I find a doctor?**
où est-ce que je peux trouver un médecin ?
*oo ess kuh zhuh puh troo-vay AN mayd-sAN ?*

**I'd like to make an appointment for today**
je voudrais prendre rendez-vous pour aujourd'hui
*zhu voo-dray prONdr rON-day-voo poor oh-zhoor-dwee*

**as soon as possible**
le plus tôt possible
*luh plU toh poh-seebl*

**can you send an ambulance to ...**
est-ce que vous pourriez faire venir une ambulance à/au ...
*ess kuh voo poor-yay fer vuh-neer Un ON-bU-lONs a/oh ...*

**I've lost a contact lens**
j'ai perdu une lentille
*zhay per-dU UN lON-tee*

**I've broken my glasses**
j'ai cassé mes lunettes
*zhay ka-say may lU-net*

### Understanding

**cabinet médical**
**salle d'attente**
**urgences**

doctor's surgery
waiting room
casualty department

**il n'y a rien de libre avant jeudi**
there are no appointments available until Thursday

**vendredi à 14 heures, ça vous va ?**
is Friday at 2pm OK?

## AT THE DOCTOR'S OR THE HOSPITAL

### Expressing yourself

**I have an appointment with Dr ...**
j'ai rendez-vous avec le Docteur ...
*zhay rON-day-voo a-vek luh dok-tuhr ...*

**I don't feel very well**
je me sens pas très bien
*zhu nuh muh sON pa tray byAN*

**I feel very weak**
je me sens très faible
*zhu muh sON tray febl*

HEALTH

107

**I don't know what it is**
je ne sais pas ce que c'est
zhuh nuh say pas kuh say

**I've got a headache**
j'ai mal à la tête
zhay mal a la tet

**I've got a sore throat**
j'ai mal à la gorge
zhay mal a la gorzh

**it hurts**
ça fait mal
sa fay mal

**I feel sick**
j'ai mal au cœur
zhay mal oh kuhr

**it's been three days**
ça fait trois jours
sa fay trwa zhoor

**I've been bitten/stung by …**
j'ai été mordu/piqué par …
zhay ay-tay mor-dU/pee-kay par …

**I've got toothache/stomachache**
j'ai mal aux dents/au ventre
zhay mal oh dON/oh vONtr

**my back hurts**
j'ai mal au dos
zhay mal oh doh

**it hurts here**
ça fait mal ici
sa fay mal ee-see

**it's got worse**
ça s'est aggravé
sa say a-gra-vay

**it started last night**
ça a commencé la nuit dernière
sa a koh-mON-say la nwee der-nyer

**it's never happened to me before**
ça ne m'était jamais arrivé avant
sa ne may-tay zha-may a-ree-vay a-vON

**I've got a temperature**
j'ai de la fièvre
zhay duh la fee-yevr

**I have a heart condition**
je suis cardiaque
zhuh swee kar-dyak

**I have asthma**
j'ai de l'asthme
zhay duh lasm

**I've been on antibiotics for a week and I'm not getting any
  better**
je suis sous antibiotiques depuis une semaine et ça ne va pas mieux
zhuh swee sooz ON-tee-byoh-teek duh-pwee Un suh-men ay sa nuh va pa
myuh

**it itches**
ça démange
sa day-mONzh

**I'm on the pill**
je prends la pilule
zhuh prON la pee-lUl

**I'm ... months pregnant**
je suis enceinte de ... mois
*zhuh sweez ON-sANt duh ... mwa*

**I'm allergic to penicillin**
je suis allergique à la pénicilline
*zhuh sweez a-ler-zheek a la pay-nee-see-leen*

**I've twisted my ankle**
je me suis tordu la cheville
*zhuh muh swee tor-dU la shuh-vee*

**I've lost a filling**
j'ai perdu un plombage
*zhay per-dU AN plON-bazh*

**is it contagious?**
c'est contagieux ?
*say kON-ta-zhyuh ?*

**how much do I owe you?**
combien je vous dois ?
*kON-byAN zh-voo dwa ?*

**I've had a blackout**
je me suis évanoui
*zhuh muh sweez ay-va-nwee*

**I fell and hurt my back**
je suis tombé sur le dos
*zhuh swee tON-bay sUr luh doh*

**is it serious?**
c'est grave ?
*say grav ?*

**how is he/she?**
comment va-t-il/va-t-elle ?
*koh-mON va-teel/va-tel ?*

## Understanding

**si vous voulez bien patientez dans la salle d'attente ...**
if you'd like to take a seat in the waiting room ...

**où est-ce que vous avez mal ?**
where does it hurt?

**respirez bien fort**
take a deep breath

**allongez-vous, s'il vous plaît**
lie down, please

**êtes-vous allergique à ... ?**
are you allergic to ...?

**est-ce que ça fait mal quand j'appuie ici ?**
does it hurt when I press here?

**est-ce que vous êtes vacciné contre ... ?**
have you been vaccinated against ...?

**avez-vous des traitements en cours ?**
are you taking any other medication?

**je vais vous faire une ordonnance**
I'm going to write you a prescription

**ça devrait passer en quelques jours**
it should clear up in a few days

**ça devrait cicatriser rapidement**
it should heal quickly

**il va falloir opérer**
you're going to need an operation

**revenez me voir dans une semaine**
come back and see me in a week

# AT THE CHEMIST'S

### Expressing yourself

**I'd like a box of plasters, please**
je voudrais une boîte de pansements, s'il vous plaît
*zhuh voo-dray Un bwat duh pONs-mON, seel voo play*

**could I have something for a bad cold?**
est-ce que vous pourriez me donner quelque chose contre le rhume ?
*ess kuh voo poor-yay muh doh-nay kel-kuh shohz kON-truh luh rUm ?*

**I need something for a cough**
j'ai besoin de quelque chose contre la toux
*zhay buh-zwAN duh kel-kuh shohz kON-truh la too*

**I'm allergic to aspirin**
je suis allergique à l'aspirine
*zhuh sweez a-ler-zheek a las-pee-reen*

**I need the morning-after pill**
j'aurais besoin de la pilule du lendemain
*zhoh-ray buh-zwAN duh la pee-lUl dU lON-duh-mAN*

**I'd like to try a homeopathic remedy**
je voudrais essayer de prendre de l'homéopathie
*zhuh voo-dray ay-say-yay duh prONdr duh loh-may-oh-pa-tee*

**I'd like a bottle of solution for soft contact lenses**
je voudrais une solution de nettoyage pour lentilles souples
*zhuh voo-dray Un soh-lUs-yON duh nay-twa-yazh poor lOn-tee soopl*

## Understanding

| | |
|---|---|
| **appliquer** | apply |
| **à prendre trois fois par jour avant les repas** | take three times a day before meals |
| **comprimé** | tablet |
| **contre-indications** | contra-indications |
| **crème** | cream |
| **effervescent** | effervescent |
| **effets secondaires éventuels** | possible side effects |
| **en poudre** | powder |
| **gélule** | capsule |
| **notice** | directions for use |
| **podologie** | dosage |
| **pommade** | ointment |
| **sirop** | syrup |
| **suppositoires** | suppositories |
| **uniquement sur ordonnance** | available on prescription only |

---

### Some informal expressions

**être cloué au lit** to be stuck in bed
**tomber dans les pommes** to pass out
**être patraque** to feel under the weather
**être barbouillé** to feel queasy

# PROBLEMS AND EMERGENCIES

Look out for pickpockets, particularly in tourist areas.

If you lose something in a station etc, go to lost property (**objets trouvés**). Otherwise go to the nearest police station (**commissariat** or **gendarmerie**).

In an emergency, dial **17** for **police secours**, a centralized service which takes calls and coordinates the appropriate response. The police in France wear dark blue uniforms and are divided into various services with different responsibilities. To call the fire brigade (**pompiers**), dial **18**. Dial **15** for emergency medical services (**SAMU**).

## The basics

| | |
|---|---|
| accident | accident *ak-see-dON* |
| ambulance | ambulance *ON-bU-lONs* |
| coastguard | gendarmerie maritime *zhON-dar-muh-ree ma-ree-teem* |
| disabled | handicapé *ON-dee-ka-pay* |
| doctor | médecin *mayd-sAN* |
| emergency | urgence *Ur-zhONs* |
| fire brigade | pompiers *pON-pyay* |
| hospital | hôpital *oh-pee-tal* |
| ill | malade *ma-lad* |
| injured | blessé *blay-say* |
| police | police *poh-lees* |

## Expressing yourself

**can you help me?**
est-ce que vous pourriez m'aider ?
*ess kuh voo poor-yay may-day ?*

**help!**
au secours !
*ohs-koor !*

**be careful!**
attention !
*a-tONs-yON !*

**it's an emergency!**
c'est urgent !
*set Ur-zhON !*

**there's been an accident**
il y a eu un accident
*eel ya U ANn ak-see-dON*

**could I use your mobile, please?**
excusez-moi, est-ce que je pourrais utiliser votre portable ?
*eks-kU-zay mwa, ess kuh zhuh poo-ray U-tee-lee-zay vo-truh por-tabl ?*

**does anyone here speak English?**
est-ce que quelqu'un parle anglais ?
*ess kuh kel-kAN parl ON-glay ?*

**I need to contact the British consulate**
je dois contacter le consulat britannique
*zhuh dwa kON-tak-tay luh kON-sU-la bree-ta-neek*

**where's the nearest police station?**
où est le commissariat le plus proche ?
*oo ay luh koh-mee-sa-rya luh plU prosh ?*

**what do I have to do?**
qu'est-ce que je dois faire ?
*kess kuh zhuh dwa fer ?*

**my bag's been stolen**
on m'a volé mon sac
*ON ma voh-lay mON sak*

**my passport/credit card has been stolen**
on m'a volé mon passeport/ma carte de crédit
*ON ma voh-lay mON pas-por/ma kart duh kray-dee*

**I've lost ...**
j'ai perdu ...
*zhay per-dU ...*

**I've been attacked**
j'ai été agressé
*zhay ay-tay a-gray-say*

**my son/daughter is missing**
mon fils/ma fille a disparu
*mON fees/ma fee a dees-pa-rU*

**I've broken down**
je suis en panne
*zhuh sweez ON pan*

**my car's been towed away**
ma voiture a été emmenée à la fourrière
*ma wwa-tUr a ay-tay ONm-nay a la foo-ryer*

**my car's been broken into**
on a forcé la porte/le coffre de ma voiture
*ONn a for-say la port/luh kofr duh ma vwa-tUr*

**there's a man following me**
il y a un homme qui me suit
*eel ya ANn om kee muh swee*

**is there disabled access?**
est-ce qu'il y a un accès pour handicapés ?
*ess keel ya ANn ak-se poor ON-dee-ka-pay ?*

**can you keep an eye on my things for a minute?**
pouvez-vous surveiller mes affaires un instant ?
*poo-vay voo sUr-vay-yay mayz a-fer ANn AN-stON ?*

## Understanding

| | |
|---|---|
| **attention au chien** | beware of the dog |
| **commissariat** | police station |
| **gendarmerie** | police station |
| **objets trouvés** | lost property |
| **police-secours** | police emergency services |
| **SAMU** | emergency medical services |
| **secours de montagne** | mountain rescue |
| **service de dépannage** | breakdown service |
| **sortie de secours** | emergency exit |

# POLICE

## Expressing yourself

**I want to report something stolen**
je voudrais faire une déclaration de vol
*zhuh voo-dray fer Un day-kla-ras-yON duh vol*

**I need a document from the police for my insurance company**
j'ai besoin d'un certificat de police pour ma compagnie d'assurances
*zhay buh-zwAN dAN ser-tee-fee-ka duh poh-lees poor ma kON-pa-nee da-sU-rONs*

## Understanding

**Filling in forms**

**nom de famille** surname
**nom de jeune fille** maiden name
**prénoms** first names
**date de naissance** date of birth
**lieu de naissance** place of birth
**sexe: H/F** sex: M/F
**nationalité** nationality
**adresse** address
**code postal** postcode
**pays** country
**durée du séjour** duration of stay
**date d'arrivée/de départ** arrival/departure date
**profession** occupation
**numéro de passeport** passport number

**qu'est-ce qu'il vous manque ?**
what's missing?

**quand cela s'est-il passé ?**
when did this happen?

**où logez-vous ?**
where are you staying?

**pouvez-vous le/la décrire ?**
can you describe him/her/it?

**je vais vous demander de remplir ce formulaire**
would you fill in this form, please?

**une signature ici, s'il vous plaît**
would you sign here, please?

**Some informal expressions**

**flic** cop
**taule** jail
**on m'a piqué mon portefeuille** my wallet's been nicked
**il s'est fait pincer** he got nicked

# TIME AND DATE

## The basics

| | |
|---|---|
| after | après *a-pray* |
| afternoon | après-midi *a-pray-mee-dee* |
| already | déjà *day-zha* |
| always | toujours *too-zhoor* |
| at lunchtime | à l'heure du déjeuner *a luhr dU day-zh-nay* |
| at the moment | en ce moment *ON suh moh-mON* |
| before | avant *a-vON* |
| between ... and ... | entre ... et ... *ONtr ... ay ...* |
| day | jour *zhoor* |
| during | pendant *pON-dON* |
| early | tôt *toh* |
| evening | soir *swar* |
| for a long time | longtemps *lON-tON* |
| from ... to ... | de ... à ... *duh ... a ...* |
| from time to time | de temps en temps *duh tOnz ON tON* |
| in a little while | d'ici peu *dee-see puh* |
| in the evening | dans la soirée *dON la swa-ray* |
| last | dernier *der-nyay* |
| late | tard *tar* |
| morning | matin *ma-tAN* |
| month | mois *mwa* |
| never | jamais *zha-may* |
| next | prochain *pro-shAN* |
| night | nuit *nwee* |
| not yet | pas encore *paz ON-kor* |
| now | maintenant *mAN-tuh-nON* |
| occasionally | de temps en temps *duh tOnz ON tON* |
| often | souvent *soo-vON* |
| rarely | rarement *rar-mON* |
| recently | récemment *ray-sa-mON* |
| since | depuis *duh-pwee* |
| sometimes | quelquefois *kel-kuh-fwa* |
| soon | bientôt *byAN-toh* |
| still | encore *ON-kor*, toujours *too-zhoor* |

| | |
|---|---|
| **straightaway** | **tout de suite** *toot sweet* |
| **until** | **jusqu'à** *zhUs-ka* |
| **week** | **semaine** *suh-men* |
| **weekend** | **week-end** *wee-kend* |
| **year** | **an** *ON* |

## Expressing yourself

**see you soon!**
à bientôt !
*a byAN-toh !*

**see you later!**
à plus tard !
*a plU tar !*

**see you on Monday!**
à lundi !
*a lAN-dee !*

**have a good weekend!**
bon week-end !
*bON wee-kend !*

**sorry I'm late**
désolé d'être en retard
*day-zoh-lay detr ON ruh-tar*

**I haven't been there yet**
je n'y ai pas encore été
*zhuh ny-ay paz ON-kor ay-tay*

**I haven't had time to …**
je n'ai pas eu le temps de …
*zhuh nay paz U luh tON duh …*

**I've got plenty of time**
j'ai tout mon temps
*zhay too mON tON*

**I'm in a rush**
je suis pressé
*zhuh swee pray-say*

**hurry up!**
dépêche-toi !/dépêchez-vous !
*day-pesh-twa !/day-pay-shay voo !*

**just a minute, please**
un instant, s'il vous plaît
*ANn AN-stAN, seel voo play*

**I had a late night**
je me suis couché tard
*zhuh muh swee koo-shay tar*

**I got up very early**
je me suis levé très tôt
*zhuh muh swee luh-vay tray toh*

**I waited ages**
j'ai attendu une éternité
*zhay a-tON-dU Un ay-ter-nee-tay*

**I have to get up very early tomorrow to catch my plane**
je dois me lever très tôt demain pour prendre l'avion
*zhuh dwa muh luh-vay tray toh duh-mAN poor prONdr lav-yON*

**we only have four days left**
il ne nous reste que quatre jours
*eel nuh noo rest kuh katr zhoor*

# THE DATE

You can write the date in figures as in English eg 04/04/06. When written out in full with the day of the week or when spoken it is: **le dimanche quatre avril.** Note that French uses cardinal not ordinal numbers, so, in English "the fourth of April" and in French **le quatre avril.** The exception to this is the first of every month, where the ordinal is used: **le 1ᵉʳ mai** (le premier mai).

## The basics

| | |
|---|---|
| **at the beginning of** | au début de *oh day-bU duh* |
| **at the end of** | à la fin de *a la fAN duh* |
| **in the middle of** | en milieu de *ON meel-yuh duh* |
| **in two days' time** | dans deux jours *dON duh zhoor* |
| **last night** | hier soir *ee-yer swar* |
| **the day after tomorrow** | après-demain *a-pray duh-mAN* |
| **the day before yesterday** | avant-hier *a-vON tee-yer* |
| **today** | aujourd'hui *oh-zhoor-dwee* |
| **tomorrow** | demain *duh-mAN* |
| **tomorrow morning/afternoon/ evening** | demain matin/après-midi/soir *duh-mAN ma-tAN/a-pray-mee-dee/swar* |
| **yesterday** | hier *ee-yer* |
| **yesterday morning/afternoon/ evening** | hier matin/après-midi/soir *ee-yer ma-tAN/a-pray-mee-dee/swar* |

## Expressing yourself

**I was born in 1975**
je suis né en 1975
*zhuh swee nay ON meel nuhf sON swa-sONt kANz*

**I came here a few years ago**
je suis venu ici il y a quelques années
*zhuh swee vuh-nU ee-see eel ya kel-kuhz a-nay*

**I spent a month in France last summer**
j'ai passé un mois en France l'été dernier
*zhay pa-say AN mwa ON frONs lay-tay der-nyay*

**I was here last year at the same time**
j'étais ici l'an dernier à la même époque
*jay-tay ee-see lON der-nyay a la mem ay-pok*

**what's the date today?**
on est le combien aujourd'hui ?
*ONn ay luh kON-byAN oh-zhoor-dwee ?*

**what day is it today?**
quel jour on est aujourd'hui ?
*kel zhoor ONn ay oh-zhoor-dwee ?*

**it's the 1st of May**
on est le premier mai
*ONn ay luh pruh-myay may*

**I'm staying until Sunday**
je suis ici jusqu'à dimanche
*zhuh sweez ee-see zhUs-ka dee-mONsh*

**we're leaving tomorrow**
nous partons demain
*noo par-tON duh-mAN*

**I already have plans for Tuesday**
j'ai déjà quelque chose de prévu mardi
*zhay day-zha kel-kuh shohz duh pray-vU mar-dee*

## Understanding

**une/deux fois**
once/twice

**trois fois par heure/jour**
three times an hour/a day

**tous les jours/lundis**
every day/Monday

**ça a été construit au milieu du dix-neuvième siècle**
it was built in the mid-nineteenth century

**il y a beaucoup de monde ici en été**
it gets very busy here in the summer

**vous êtes arrivé quand ?**
when did you get here?

**vous êtes ici pour combien temps ?**
how long are you staying?

**quand est-ce que vous partez ?**
when are you leaving?

# THE TIME

The twenty-four hour clock is commonly used in France, so you will hear people say **il est quatorze heures** for "it's 2 o'clock" (in the afternoon).

However, it is also acceptable to use the twelve-hour clock, if necessary adding **du matin** (in the morning, used until midday), **de l'après-midi** (in the afternoon, used until 5pm) or **du soir** (in the evening/at night, used for the rest of the evening).

## The basics

| | |
|---|---|
| early | tôt *toh* |
| half an hour | une demi-heure *Un duh-mee uhr* |
| in the afternoon | de l'après-midi *duh la-pray-mee-dee* |
| in the morning | du matin *dU ma-tAN* |
| late | tard *tar* |
| midday | midi *mee-dee* |
| midnight | minuit *meen-wee* |
| on time | à l'heure *a luhr* |
| quarter of an hour | quart d'heure *kar duhr* |
| three quarters of an hour | trois quarts d'heure *trwa kar duhr* |

## Expressing yourself

**what time is it?**
quelle heure est-il ?
*kel uhr ay-teel ?*

**it's exactly three o'clock**
il est trois/quinze heures pile
*eel ay trwaz/kANz uhr peel*

**excuse me, have you got the time, please?**
excusez-moi, est-ce que vous auriez l'heure ?
*eks-kU-zay-mwa, ess kuh vooz oh-ryay luhr ?*

**it's nearly one o'clock**
il est presque une heure/presque treize heures
*eel ay presk Un uhr/preskuh trez uhr*

**it's twenty past twelve**
il est midi vingt
*eel ay mee-dee vAN*

**it's ten past one**
il est une heure/treize heures dix
*eel ay Un uhr/trez uhr dees*

**it's a quarter past one**
il est une heure et quart/treize heures quinze
*eel ay Un uhr ay kar/trez uhr kANz*

**it's a quarter to one**
il est une heure moins le quart/douze heures quarante-cinq
*eel ay Un uhr mwAN luh kar/dooz uhr ka-rONt-sANk*

**it's twenty to twelve**
il est midi moins vingt
*eel ay mee-dee mwAN vAN*

**it's half past one**
il est une heure et demie/treize heures trente
*eel ay Un uhr ay duh-mee/trez uhr trONt*

**I arrived at about two o'clock**
je suis arrivé vers deux heures
*zhuh sweez a-ree-vay ver duhz uhr*

**I set my alarm for nine**
j'ai mis mon réveil à neuf heures
*zhay mee mON ray-vey a nuhv uhr*

**I waited twenty minutes**
j'ai attendu vingt minutes
*zhay a-tON-dU vAN mee-nUt*

**the train was fifteen minutes late**
le train a eu quinze minutes de retard
*le trAN a U kANz mee-nUt duh ruh-tar*

**I got home an hour ago**
je suis arrivé à la maison il y a une heure
*zhuh sweez a-ree-vay a la may-zON eel ya Un uhr*

**shall we meet in half an hour?**
on se retrouve dans une demi-heure ?
*ON suh ruh-troov dONz Un duh-mee uhr ?*

**I'll be back in a quarter of an hour**
je serai de retour dans un quart d'heure
*zhuh suh-ray duh ruh-toor dONz AN kar duhr*

**there's a one-hour time difference between … and …**
il y a une heure de décalage entre … et …
*eel ya Un uhr duh day-ka-lazh ONtr … ay …*

## Understanding

**ouvert de 10h à 19h**            open from 10am to 7pm

**ça joue tous les soirs à 20h**
it's on every evening at eight

**ça dure environ une heure et demie**
it lasts around an hour and a half

**ça ouvre à 10h**
it opens at ten in the morning

---

**Some informal expressions**

**à deux heures pile** at two o'clock on the dot
**être à la bourre** to be late, to be in a big rush
**grouille-toi !** get a move on!

# NUMBERS

**0** zéro *zay-roh*
**1** un *AN*
**2** deux *duh*
**3** trois *trwa*
**4** quatre *katr*
**5** cinq *sANk*
**6** six *sees*
**7** sept *set*
**8** huit *weet*
**9** neuf *nuhf*
**10** dix *dees*
**11** onze *ONz*
**12** douze *dooz*
**13** treize *trez*
**14** quatorze *ka-torz*
**15** quinze *kANz*
**16** seize *sez*
**17** dix-sept *dees-set*
**18** dix-huit *deez-weet*
**19** dix-neuf *deez-nuhf*
**20** vingt *vAN*
**21** vingt et un *vAN-tay-AN*
**22** vingt-deux *vANt-duh*
**30** trente *trONt*
**35** trente-cinq *trONt-sANk*

**40** quarante *ka-rONt*
**50** cinquante *sAN-kONt*
**60** soixante *swa-sONt*
**70** soixante-dix *swa-sONt-dees*
**80** quatre-vingts *ka-truh-vAN*
**90** quatre-vingt-dix *ka-truh-vAN-dees*
**100** cent *sON*
**101** cent un *sON-AN*
**200** deux cents *duh sON*
**500** cinq cents *sANk sON*
**1000** mille *meel*
**2000** deux mille *duh meel*
**10 000** dix mille *dee meel*
**1 000 000** un million *AN meel-yON*

**first** premier *pruhm-yay*
**second** deuxième *duhz-yem*
**third** troisième *trwaz-yem*
**fourth** quatrième *ka-tree-yem*
**fifth** cinquième *sANk-yem*
**sixth** sixième *seez-yem*
**seventh** septième *set-yem*
**eighth** huitième *weet-yem*
**ninth** neuvième *nuhv-yem*
**tenth** dixième *deez-yem*
**twentieth** vingtième *vANt-yem*

**20 plus 3 equals 23**
vingt plus trois égale vingt-trois
*vAN plUs trwa ay-gal vANt-trwa*

**20 minus 3 equals 17**
vingt moins trois égale dix-sept
*vAN mwAN trwa ay-gal dees-set*

**20 multiplied by 4 equals 80**
vingt multiplié par quatre égale quatre-vingts
*vAN mUl-tee-plee-yay par katr ay-gal ka-truh-vAN*

**20 divided by 4 equals 5**
vingt divisé par quatre égale cinq
*vAN dee-vee-zay par katr ay-gal sANk*

# DICTIONARY

## ENGLISH-FRENCH

### A

**a** un(e) *(see grammar)*
**abbey** abbaye *f*
**able: to be able to** pouvoir
**about** environ; **to be about to do** être sur le point de faire
**above** au-dessus (de), dessus
**abroad** à l'étranger
**accept** accepter
**access** accès *m* 114
**accident** accident *m* 30, 113
**accommodation** logement *mf*
**across** à travers
**adaptor** adaptateur *m*
**address** adresse *f* 18
**addressee** destinataire *mf*
**admission** entrée *f* 70
**advance: in advance** à l'avance 64
**advice** conseils *mpl*; **to ask somebody's advice** demander conseil à quelqu'un
**advise** conseiller
**affordable** abordable
**Africa** Afrique *f*
**after** après
**afternoon** après-midi *m or f*
**after-sun** lait *m* après-soleil
**again** encore, à nouveau
**against** contre
**age** âge *m*
**air** air *m*
**airbed** matelas *m* pneumatique
**air conditioning** climatisation *f*
**airline** compagnie *f* aérienne
**airmail** par avion

**airport** aéroport *m*
**airport tax** taxe *f* d'aéroport
**alarm clock** réveil *m*
**alcohol** alcool *m*
**alive** vivant(e)
**all** tout(e); **all day/week** toute la journée/semaine; **all inclusive** tout compris; **all the better** tant mieux; **all the same** quand même; **all the time** tout le temps
**allergic** allergique 109
**almost** presque
**already** déjà
**also** aussi
**although** quoique, bien que
**always** toujours
**ambulance** ambulance *f* 107
**American** *(n)* Américain(e) *m,f; (adj)* américain(e)
**among** parmi
**anaesthetic** anesthésie *f*
**and** et
**animal** animal *m*
**ankle** cheville *f*
**anniversary** anniversaire *m*
**another** un(e) autre
**answer** *(n)* réponse *f; (v)* répondre
**answering machine** répondeur *m*
**ant** fourmi *f*
**antibiotic** antibiotique *m*
**anybody, anyone** n'importe qui
**anything** n'importe quoi
**anyway** de toute façon, bref
**appendicitis** appendicite *f*
**appointment** rendez-vous *m* 107; **to make an appointment**

prendre un rendez-vous; **to have an appointment (with)** avoir rendez-vous (avec)

**April** avril m

**area** (of town) quartier m; (of country) région f; **in the area** dans la région

**arm** bras m

**around** (approximately) à peu près, vers

**arrange** arranger; **to arrange to meet** se donner rendez-vous

**arrival** arrivée f

**arrive** arriver

**art** art m

**art gallery** galerie f (d'art)

**artist** artiste mf

**as** comme; **as soon as possible** le plus tôt possible; **as soon as** dès que; **as well as** aussi bien que

**ashamed: to be ashamed** avoir honte

**ashtray** cendrier m **43**

**Asia** Asie f

**ask** demander; **to ask a question** poser une question

**aspirin** aspirine f

**asthma** asthme m

**at** à

**attack** (v) attaquer, agresser **113**

**auditorium** salle f de cinéma

**August** août m

**autumn** automne m

**available** libre, disponible

**avenue** avenue f

**away: 2 km away** à 2 km

---

**B**

**baby** bébé m

**baby's bottle** biberon m

**babysitter** baby-sitter mf

**back** dos m; **at the back of** au fond de; **to be back** être de retour

**backpack** sac m à dos

**bad** mauvais; mal

**bag** sac m

**baggage** bagages mpl

**baggage reclaim** retrait m des bagages

**bake** cuire (au four)

**baker's** boulangerie f

**balcony** balcon m

**ball** (large) ballon m, (small) balle f

**bandage** bandage m

**bank** banque f **92**

**bank account** compte m bancaire

**banknote** billet m

**bar** bar m

**barbecue** barbecue m

**bath** bain m; **to have a bath** prendre un bain

**bathroom** salle f de bains

**battery** batterie f, pile f

**be** être

**beach** plage f

**beach umbrella** parasol m

**beard** barbe f

**beautiful** beau m, belle f

**bed** lit m; **to go to bed** aller se coucher, aller au lit

**bed and breakfast** chambres fpl d'hôte

**bee** abeille f

**before** avant; **before doing…** avant de faire…

**begin** commencer

**beginner** débutant(e) m,f

**beginning** début m; **at the beginning** au début

**behind** derrière

**Belgian** (n) Belge mf; (adj) belge

**Belgium** Belgique f

**believe** croire

**below** en dessous (de)

**beside** à côté de

**best** meilleur(e) m,f; **the best** le meilleur m, la meilleure f; **best wishes** meilleurs vœux; **all the best!** bonne continuation!

**better** (adj) meilleur(e); **better than…** meilleur(e) que…

**better** *(adv)* mieux; **better than…** mieux que…; **to get better** s'améliorer; guérir; **it's better to…** il vaut mieux…

**between** entre

**bicycle** bicyclette *f*

**bicycle pump** pompe *f* à vélo

**big** grand(e), gros *m*, grosse *f*

**bike** vélo *m*

**bill** facture *f*; *(in restaurant)* addition *f*, note *f* **48**

**bin** poubelle *f*

**binoculars** jumelles *fpl*

**birthday** anniversaire *m*

**bit** bout *m*, morceau *m*

**bite** *(n)* morsure *f*; *(v)* mordre

**black** *(adj)* noir(e); *(n)* noir *m*; **black and white** noir et blanc

**blanket** couverture *f*

**bleed** saigner

**bless: bless you!** à tes/vos souhaits!

**blind** aveugle

**blister** ampoule *f*

**blond** blond

**blonde** blonde

**blood** sang *m*

**blood pressure** tension *f*

**blue** *(adj)* bleu(e); *(n)* bleu *m*

**board** embarquer **25**

**boarding** embarquement *m*

**boat** bateau *m*

**body** corps *m*

**book** *(n)* livre *m*; **book of tickets** carnet *m* de tickets

**book** *(v)* réserver **31**

**bookshop** librairie *m*

**boot** *(footwear)* botte *f*; *(of car)* coffre *m*

**borrow** emprunter

**boss** patron *m*, patronne *f*, chef *m*

**botanical garden** jardin *m* botanique

**both** tous les deux *m*, toutes les deux *f*

**bottle** bouteille *f*; *(baby's)* biberon *m*

**bottle opener** décapsuleur *m*, ouvre-bouteilles *m*

**bottom** fond *m*; *(buttocks)* fesses *fpl*; **at the bottom** en bas; **at the bottom of** au fond de

**bowl** bol *m*

**boxer shorts** caleçon *m*

**boy** garçon *m*

**boyfriend** petit ami *m*, *(informal)* (petit) copain *m*

**bra** soutien-gorge *m*

**brake** *(n)* frein *m*; *(v)* freiner

**bread** pain *m*

**break** casser; **to break one's leg** se casser la jambe

**break down** tomber en panne **30, 113**

**breakdown** panne *f*

**breakdown service** service *m* de dépannage

**breakfast** petit déjeuner *m* **36**; **to have breakfast** prendre le petit déjeuner

**bridge** pont *m*

**bring** apporter, amener

**brochure** brochure *f*

**broken** cassé(e)

**bronchitis** bronchite *f*

**brother** frère *m*

**brown** *(adj)* marron; *(n)* marron *m*

**brush** brosse *f*

**build** construire

**building** bâtiment *m*

**bump** bosse *f*

**bumper** pare-chocs *m*

**buoy** bouée *f*

**burn** *(n)* brûlure *f*

**burn** *(v)* brûler; **to burn oneself** se brûler

**burst** *(v)* crever; *(adj)* crevé(e)

**bus** autobus *m*, bus *m* **28**

**bus route** ligne *f* de bus

**bus stop** arrêt *m* de bus

**business** affaires *fpl*; **on business** pour affaires

**business card** carte *f* de visite

**business class** classe *f* affaires

**business trip** voyage *m* d'affaires

**busy** occupé(e), animé(e)
**but** mais
**butcher's** boucherie *f*
**buy** acheter **82**, **84**
**by** par; **by car** en voiture; **by the way…** au fait,…
**bye!** au revoir !, *(informal)* salut !

## C

**café** café *m*
**call** *(n)* appel *m*; *(v)* appeler **103**
**call back** rappeler
**camera** appareil *m* photo; *(video)* caméra *f*
**camper** camping-car *m*
**camping** camping *m*; **to go camping** faire du camping **40**
**camping stove** camping-gaz® *m*
**campsite** (terrain *m* de) camping *m*
**can** *(n)* boîte *f* (de conserve)
**can** *(v)* pouvoir; **can you swim?** est-ce que tu sais nager?; **I can't** je ne peux pas
**can opener** ouvre-boîtes *m*
**cancel** annuler
**candle** bougie *f*
**car** voiture *f*; **by car** en voiture
**caravan** caravane *f*
**card** carte *f*
**car park** parking *m*
**carry** porter
**case: in case of…** en cas de…
**cash** liquide *m*; **to pay cash** payer en liquide
**cashpoint** distributeur *m* (automatique de billets) **92**
**castle** château *m*
**catch** attraper
**cathedral** cathédrale *f*
**cavity: to have a cavity** avoir une carie
**CD** CD *m*
**cemetery** cimetière *m*

**centimetre** centimètre *m*
**centre** centre *m* **36**
**century** siècle *m*
**chair** chaise *f*
**chairlift** télésiège *m*
**chance** hasard *m*; **by chance** par hasard
**change** *(n)* changement *m*; monnaie *f* **82**, **83**; *(v)* changer **92**
**changing room** cabine *f* d'essayage **86**
**channel** *(TV)* chaîne *f*; **the (English) Channel** la Manche
**chapel** chapelle *f*
**charge** *(money)* faire payer; *(battery)* recharger
**cheap** bon marché
**check** *(v)* vérifier
**check in** enregistrer
**check-in** enregistrement *m* **25**
**checkout** caisse *f*
**cheers!** *(when drinking)* santé!; *(thanks)* merci!
**chemist's** pharmacie *f*
**cheque** chèque *m*
**chest** poitrine *f*
**child** enfant *mf*
**chilly** frais *m*, fraîche *f*, froid(e)
**chimney** cheminée *f*
**chin** menton *m*
**Chinese** *(n)* Chinois(e) *m,f*; *(language)* chinois *m*; *(adj)* chinois(e)
**Christmas** Noël *m*
**church** *(Catholic)* église *f*; *(Protestant)* temple *m*
**cigar** cigare *m*
**cigarette** cigarette *f*
**cigarette paper** papier *m* à cigarette
**cinema** cinéma *m*
**circus** cirque *m*
**city** ville *f*
**class** *(lesson)* cours *m*; *(groupe)* classe *f*
**classic** classique
**classical** classique
**clean** *(adj)* propre

**clean** *(v)* nettoyer; **to clean one's teeth** se laver les dents
**clementine** clémentine *f*
**cliff** falaise *f*
**climate** climat *m*
**climbing** escalade *f*
**cloakroom** vestiaire *m*
**close** *(v)* fermer
**closed** fermé
**closing** fermeture *f*; **closing time** heure *f* de fermeture
**clothes** vêtements *mpl*
**clutch** embrayage *m*
**coach** *(bus)* autocar *m*, car *m* **28**; *(of train)* voiture *f*
**coach station** gare *f* routière
**coast** côte *f*
**coathanger** cintre *m*
**cockroach** cafard *m*
**code** code *m*
**coffee** café *m*
**coil** stérilet *m*
**coin** pièce *f*
**Coke®** Coca® *m*
**cold** *(n)* rhume *m*; **to have a cold** être enrhumé(e)
**cold** *(adj)* froid(e); **it's cold** il fait froid; **I'm cold** j'ai froid
**collection** *(of objects)* collection *f*; *(postal)* levée *f*
**colour** couleur *f*
**comb** peigne *m*
**come** venir
**come back** revenir
**come in** entrer
**come out** sortir
**comfortable** à l'aise, confortable
**comic strip** bande *f* dessinée
**company** société *f*
**compartment** compartiment *m*
**complain** se plaindre
**comprehensive insurance** assurance *f* tous risques
**computer** ordinateur *m*

**concert** concert *m* **65**
**concert hall** salle *f* de concert
**concession** tarif *m* réduit **23**, **71**
**condom** préservatif *m*
**conference** conférence *f*
**confirm** confirmer **25**
**congratulations!** félicitations !
**connection** lien *m*; *(trains, planes)* correspondance *f* **25**
**constipated** constipé(e)
**consulate** consulat *m* **113**
**contact** *(n)* contact *m*; *(v)* contacter
**contact lenses** lentilles *fpl* (de contact)
**contagious** contagieux *m*, contagieuse *f*
**contemporary** contemporain(e)
**contraceptive** contraceptif *m*
**cook** *(v)* cuisiner; *(a dish)* (faire) cuire
**cook** *(n)* cuisinier *m*, cuisinière *f*
**cooked** cuit(e)
**cooking** cuisine *f*; **to do the cooking** faire la cuisine
**cool** frais *m*, fraîche *f*; *(trendy)* branché(e)
**corkscrew** tire-bouchon *m*
**corn** maïs *m*
**correct** correct(e)
**cost** coûter
**cotton** coton *m*
**cotton bud** coton-tige® *m*
**cotton wool** coton *m*
**couchette** couchette *f*
**cough** *(n)* toux *f*; **to have a cough** avoir de la toux
**cough** *(v)* tousser
**count** compter
**count on** compter sur
**country** pays *m*; *(countryside)* campagne *f*
**countryside** campagne *f*
**course: of course** bien sûr
**cover** *(n)* couverture *f*; *(v)* couvrir
**credit card** carte *f* de crédit **35**, **48**
**crisis** crise *f*
**cross** *(n)* croix *f*; *(v)* traverser
**cruise** croisière *f*

**cry** *(v)* pleurer
**culture** culture *f*
**cup** tasse *f* **47**
**currency** devise *f*
**customs** douane *f*
**cut** couper; **to cut oneself** se couper
**cycle path** piste *f* cyclable **77**

# D

**damaged** abîmé(e)
**damp** humide
**dance** *(n)* danse *f*; *(v)* danser
**dangerous** dangereux *m*, dangereuse *f*
**dark** foncé(e); **dark blue** bleu foncé;
  **in the dark** dans le noir
**date** *(n)* date *f*; rendez-vous *m*; **out
  of date** périmé(e); **what's today's
  date?** on est le combien?
**date (from)** *(v)* dater (de)
**date of birth** date *f* de naissance
**daughter** fille *f*
**daughter-in-law** belle-fille *f*
**day** jour *m*, journée *f*; **the day after
  tomorrow** après-demain; **the day
  before yesterday** avant-hier
**dead** mort(e)
**deaf** sourd(e)
**dear** cher *m*, chère *f*
**debit card** carte *f* bancaire
**December** décembre *m*
**declare** déclarer
**deep** profond(e)
**degree** degré *m*
**delay** retard *m*
**delayed** retardé(e)
**deli** épicerie *f* fine
**dentist** dentiste *mf*
**deodorant** déodorant *m*
**department** rayon *m*
**department store** grand magasin *m*
**departure** départ *m*
**depend: it depends (on)** ça dépend (de)
**deposit** caution *f*

**desert** désert *m*
**deckchair** transat *m*
**dessert** dessert *m* **45**
**develop: to get a film developed**
  faire développer une pellicule
**diabetes** diabète *m*
**dialling code** indicatif *m*
**diarrhoea: to have diarrhoea** avoir
  la diarrhée
**dice** dé *m*
**die** mourir
**diesel** diesel *m*
**diet** régime *m*; **to be on a diet** être
  au régime
**different (from)** différent(e) (de)
**difficult (to)** difficile (à)
**dinner** dîner *m*; **to have dinner** dîner
**direct** direct(e)
**direction** direction *f*, sens *m*; **to have
  a good sense of direction** avoir le
  sens de l'orientation
**directory** annuaire *m*
**directory enquiries** les
  renseignements *mpl*
**dirty** *(adj)* sale; **to get dirty** se salir
**disabled** handicapé(e) **114**
**disappointed** déçu(e)
**disappointing** décevant(e)
**disaster** catastrophe *f*
**discount** rabais *m* **70**; **to give
  somebody a discount** faire un rabais
  à quelqu'un
**discount fare** tarif *m* réduit
**dish** plat *m*
**dishes** vaisselle *f*; **to do the dishes**
  faire la vaisselle
**dish towel** torchon *m*
**dishwasher** lave-vaisselle *m*
**disinfect** désinfecter
**disposable** jetable
**disturb** déranger
**dive** plonger
**diving** plongée *f*; **to go diving** faire de
  la plongée

**do** faire; **do you have a light?** tu as du feu?
**doctor** médecin *m*, docteur *m* **106**, **107**
**door** porte *f*
**door code** code *m* d'entrée
**downstairs** en bas
**draught beer** pression *f*
**dream** *(n)* rêve *m*; *(v)* rêver
**dress** *(n)* robe *f*
**dress:** *(v)* **to get dressed** s'habiller
**dressing** pansement *m*
**drink** *(n)* boisson *f*; **to go for a drink** aller prendre un verre **43**, **66**; **to have a drink** prendre un verre
**drink** *(v)* boire
**drinking water** eau *f* potable
**drive:** *(n)* **to go for a drive** faire un tour (en voiture)
**drive** *(v)* conduire
**driving licence** permis *m* de conduire
**drops** gouttes *fpl*
**drown** se noyer
**drug** drogue *f*
**drunk** soûl(e)
**dry** *(adj)* sec *m*, sèche *f*; *(v)* (faire) sécher
**dry cleaner's** pressing *m*
**duck** canard *m*
**during** pendant; **during the week** en semaine
**dustbin** poubelle *f*
**Dutch** *(n)* Hollandais(e) *m,f*; *(language)* hollandais *m*; *(adj)* hollandais(e)
**duty chemist's** pharmacie *f* de garde

### E

**each** chaque; **each one** chacun
**ear** oreille *f*
**early** en avance, tôt
**earplugs** boules *fpl* Quiès®
**earrings** boucles *fpl* d'oreilles
**earth** terre *f*
**Earth** la Terre

**east** est *m*; **in the east** à l'est; **(to the) east of** à l'est de
**Easter** Pâques
**easy (to)** facile (à)
**eat** manger **43**
**economy class** classe *f* économique
**egg** œuf *m*
**Elastoplast®** pansement *m*
**electric** électrique
**electric shaver** rasoir *m* électrique
**electricity** électricité *f*
**electricity meter** compteur *m* électrique
**e-mail** e-mail *m* **98**
**e-mail address** adresse *f* e-mail **18**, **98**
**embassy** ambassade *f*
**emergency** urgence *f*; **in an emergency** en cas d'urgence
**emergency exit** sortie *f* de secours
**empty** vide
**end** fin *f*; **at the end of** à la fin de; **at the end of the street** au bout de la rue
**engaged** occupé(e); **to be engaged** *(couple)* être fiancés
**engine** moteur *m*
**England** Angleterre *f*
**English** *(n)* Anglais(e) *m,f*; *(language)* anglais *m*; *(adj)* anglais(e)
**enjoy: enjoy your meal!** bon appétit!; **to enjoy oneself** bien s'amuser
**enough** assez (de); **that's enough** ça suffit
**entrance** entrée *f*
**envelope** enveloppe *f*
**epileptic** épileptique
**equipment** matériel *m*
**espresso** express *m*
**euro** euro *m*
**Eurocheque** eurochèque *m*
**Europe** Europe *f*
**European** *(n)* Européen(ne) *m,f*; *(adj)* européen *m*, européenne *f*
**European Union** Union *f* européenne

**evening** soir *m*, soirée *f*; **in the evening** dans la soirée; **in the evenings** le soir
**every** tout(e); **every day** tous les jours
**everybody, everyone** tout le monde
**everywhere** partout
**except** sauf
**exceptional** exceptionnel *m*, exceptionnelle *f*
**excess** excès *m*; **excess baggage** excédent *m* de bagages
**exchange** échanger
**exchange rate** taux *m* de change
**excuse** *(n)* excuse *f*
**excuse:** *(v)* **excuse me** pardon, excusez-moi
**exhausted** épuisé(e)
**exhaust pipe** pot *m* d'échappement
**exhibition** exposition *f* **70**
**exit** sortie *f*
**expensive** cher *m*, chère *f*
**expiry date** date *f* d'expiration
**express** *(v)* exprimer; **to express oneself** s'exprimer
**expresso** express *m*
**extra** supplémentaire
**eye** œil *m*

## F

**face** *(n)* visage *m*
**facecloth** gant *m* de toilette
**fact** fait *m*; **in fact** en fait
**faint** s'évanouir
**fair** *(n)* foire *f*
**fair** *(adj)* juste
**fall** *(v)* tomber; **to fall asleep** s'endormir; **to fall ill** tomber malade; **to fall in love (with)** tomber amoureux (de)
**family** famille *f*
**famous** célèbre
**fan** ventilateur *m*
**far** loin; **far from** loin de
**fare** tarif *m*

**fast** vite
**fast-food restaurant** fast-food *m*
**fat** *(adj)* gras *m*, grasse *f*
**father** père *m*
**favour** service *m*; **to do somebody a favour** rendre un service à quelqu'un; **to be in favour of something** être pour quelque chose
**favourite** préféré(e)
**fax** fax *m*
**February** février *m*
**fed up: to be fed up (with)** en avoir marre (de)
**feel** *(se)* sentir **107**; **to feel good/bad** se sentir bien/mal
**feeling** sentiment *m*
**ferry** ferry *m*
**festival** festival *m*
**fetch: to go and fetch somebody/ something** aller chercher quelqu'un/ quelque chose
**fever** fièvre *f*
**few** peu (de)
**fiancé** fiancé *m*
**fiancée** fiancée *f*
**fight** bagarre *f*
**fill** remplir
**fill in/out** remplir
**fill up: to fill up with petrol** faire le plein (d'essence)
**filling** plombage *m*
**film** film *m*; *(for camera)* pellicule *f* **89**
**finally** enfin, finalement
**find** trouver
**fine** *(n)* amende *f*
**fine** *(adj)* fin(e); **I'm fine** ça va
**finger** doigt *m*
**finish** finir
**fire** feu *m*, incendie *m*; **fire!** au feu !
**fire brigade** pompiers *mpl*
**fireplace** cheminée *f*
**fireworks** feux *mpl* d'artifice
**first** premier *m*, première *f*; **first (of all)** d'abord

**first class** première classe f
**first name** prénom m
**fish** (n) poisson m; (v) pêcher
**fishmonger's** poissonnerie f
**fitting room** cabine f d'essayage
**fizzy** gazeux m, gazeuse f
**flash** flash m
**flask** gourde f
**flat** (adj) plat(e); (tyre) dégonflé(e)
**flat** (n) appartement m
**flavour** parfum m
**flaw** défaut m
**flight** vol m
**flip-flops** tongs fpl
**floor** (of building) étage m; (ground) sol m; **on the floor** par terre
**floppy (disk)** disquette f
**flu** grippe f
**flush** chasse f d'eau
**fly** (n) mouche f
**fly** (v) voler
**food** nourriture f
**food poisoning** intoxication f alimentaire
**foot** pied m
**for** pour; **for an hour** pendant une heure
**forbidden** interdit(e)
**forecast** (v) prévoir
**forehead** front m
**foreign** étranger m, étrangère f
**foreigner** étranger m, étrangère f
**forest** forêt f
**fork** fourchette f
**former** ancien m, ancienne f
**forward** (v) faire suivre
**forward** (adj) avant; **forward gear** marche avant
**four-star petrol** super m
**fracture** fracture f
**fragile** fragile
**France** France f
**free** gratuit(e) **69**; libre
**freezer** congélateur m

**French** (n) Français(e) m,f; (language) français m; (adj) français(e)
**Friday** vendredi m
**fridge** frigo m
**fried** frit(e); **fried egg** œuf m sur le plat
**friend** ami(e) m,f, (informal) copain m, copine f
**fries** frites fpl
**from** (à partir) de; **from … to …** de … à …
**front** avant; **in front of** devant
**front wheel** roue f avant
**frozen food** surgelés mpl
**fruit** fruits mpl
**fruit juice** jus m de fruit
**fry** (faire) frire
**frying pan** poêle f
**full** plein(e); (hotel etc) complet m, complète f; **full of** plein(e) de
**full board** pension f complète
**full fare, full price** plein tarif m
**funfair** fête f foraine
**fuse** fusible m

## G

**game** jeu m; (meat) gibier m
**garage** garage m **30**
**garden** jardin m
**gas** gaz m
**gas cylinder** bouteille f de gaz
**gastric flu** grippe f intestinale
**gate** barrière f; (in airport) porte f
**gauze** gaze f
**gearbox** boîte f de vitesses
**gel** gel m
**general** général(e)
**gents' (toilet)** toilettes fpl pour hommes
**German** (n) Allemand(e) m,f; (language) allemand m; (adj) allemand(e)
**Germany** Allemagne f
**get** obtenir; (receive) recevoir
**get off** descendre **28**

**get on: to get on well (with someone)** bien s'entendre (avec quelqu'un)

**get up** se lever

**gift wrap** papier m cadeau

**girl** fille f

**girlfriend** petite amie f, *(informal)* (petite) copine f

**give** donner; **to give somebody a present** offrir un cadeau à quelqu'un

**give back** rendre

**glass** verre m; **a glass of water/of wine** un verre d'eau/de vin

**glasses** lunettes fpl

**go** aller; **to go to Paris/to France** aller à Paris/en France; **I'm going home** je rentre chez moi

**go away** s'en aller

**go in** entrer

**go out** sortir; **to go out with someone** sortir avec quelqu'un

**go with** aller avec; *(accompany)* accompagner

**go without** se passer de

**golf** golf m

**golf course** terrain m de golf

**good** bon m, bonne f; bien; **good luck!** bon courage !, bonne chance !; **good morning** bonjour; **good afternoon** bonjour; **good evening** bonsoir

**goodbye** au revoir

**goodnight** bonne nuit

**goods** marchandises fpl

**Gothic** gothique

**GP** généraliste mf

**grams** grammes mpl

**grass** herbe f

**great** super

**Great Britain** Grande-Bretagne f

**Greece** Grèce f

**Greek** *(n)* Grec m, Grecque f; *(language)* grec m; *(adj)* grec m, grecque f

**green** *(adj)* vert m, verte f; *(n)* vert m

**grey** *(adj)* gris(e); *(n)* gris m

**grocer's** épicerie f

**ground** sol m; **on the ground** par terre

**ground floor** rez-de-chaussée m

**groundsheet** tapis m de sol

**grow** grandir; *(cultivate)* cultiver

**guarantee** garantie f

**guest** invité(e) m,f

**guest house** chambre f d'hôtes

**guide** guide mf **64**

**guidebook** guide m

**guided tour** visite f guidée

**gynaecologist** gynécologue mf

## H

**hair** cheveux mpl

**hairdresser** coiffeur m, coiffeuse f

**hairdrier** sèche-cheveux m

**half** *(adj)* demi; *(n)* moitié f; **half a litre/kilo** un demi-litre/-kilo; **half an hour** une demi-heure

**half-board** demi-pension f

**half-pint: a half-pint** un demi

**hand** main f

**handbag** sac m à main

**handbrake** frein m à main

**handkerchief** mouchoir m

**hand luggage** bagages mpl à main **25**

**handmade** fait(e) main

**hangover** gueule f de bois

**happen** arriver, se passer

**happy** heureux m, heureuse f; **happy birthday!** bon anniversaire !; **Happy Easter!** joyeuses Pâques !; **Happy New Year!** bonne année !

**hard** dur(e)

**hard disk** disque m dur

**hat** chapeau m

**hate** détester

**have** avoir; **to have a headache/a sore throat/a sore stomach** avoir mal à la tête/à la gorge/au ventre; **to have to** devoir

**hay fever** rhume *m* des foins
**he** il
**head** tête *f*
**headlight** phare *m*
**health** santé *f*
**hear** entendre
**heart** cœur *m*
**heart attack** crise *f* cardiaque
**heat** chaleur *f*
**heating** chauffage *m*
**heavy** lourd(e)
**hello** bonjour; *(in evening)* bonsoir; *(on telephone)* allô
**helmet** casque *m*
**help** *(n)* aide *f*, secours *m*; **to call for help** appeler au secours; **help!** au secours !
**help** *(v)* aider **112**
**her** la; lui; son, sa, ses *(see grammar)*
**herbal tea** tisane *f*
**here** ici; **here is/are** voici
**hers** le sien, la sienne, les siens/siennes *(see grammar)*
**hi!** bonjour !, *(informal)* salut !
**hi-fi** chaîne *f* (hi-fi)
**high** haut(e)
**high blood pressure** hypertension *f*
**high heels** chaussures *fpl* à talons
**high tide** marée *f* haute
**hiking** randonnée *f*; **to go hiking** faire de la randonnée
**hill** colline *f*
**hill-walking** randonnée *f* **75**; **to go hill-walking** faire de la randonnée
**him** le; lui *(see grammar)*
**himself** lui-même
**hip** hanche *f*
**hire** *(n)* location *f*; *(v)* louer **30**, **74**, **77**
**his** son, sa, ses; le sien, la sienne, les siens/siennes *(see grammar)*
**hitchhike** faire du stop
**hitchhiking** stop *m*
**hold** tenir; **hold on** *(on the phone)* ne quittez pas

**holiday(s)** vacances *fpl*; **on holiday** en vacances **17**
**holiday camp** colonie *f* de vacances
**Holland** Hollande *f*
**home** maison *f*; **at home** à la maison, chez soi; **to go home** rentrer
**homosexual** homosexuel *m*, homosexuelle *f*
**honest** honnête
**honeymoon** lune *f* de miel
**horse** cheval *m*
**hospital** hôpital *m*
**hot** chaud(e); **it's hot today** il fait chaud aujourd'hui; **hot drinks** boissons *fpl* chaudes
**hot chocolate** chocolat *m* chaud
**hotel** hôtel *m*
**hotplate** plaque *f* électrique
**hour** heure *f*; **an hour and a half** une heure et demie
**house** maison *f*
**housework** ménage *m*; **to do the housework** faire le ménage
**how** comment; **how are you?** comment allez-vous ?, ça va ?
**humour** humour *m*; **to have a good sense of humour** avoir le sens de l'humour
**hunger** faim *f*
**hungry: to be hungry** avoir faim **43**
**hurry:** *(n)* **to be in a hurry** être pressé
**hurry (up)** se dépêcher
**hurt: it hurts** ça fait mal; **my head hurts** j'ai mal à la tête
**husband** mari *m*

---

# I

**I** je; **I'm French** je suis Français(e); **I'm 22 (years old)** j'ai 22 ans
**ice** glace *f*
**ice cream** glace *f*
**ice cube** glaçon *m*

**identity card** carte f d'identité

**if** si; **if ever** si jamais

**ill** malade

**illness** maladie f

**important** important(e)

**in** dans; en; **in France/2006/English** en France/2006/anglais; **in the 19th century** au XIXᵉ siècle; **in an hour** dans une heure

**included** compris(e)

**independent** indépendant(e)

**indicator** clignotant m

**infection** infection f

**information** renseignements mpl, informations fpl **69**

**injection** piqûre f

**injured** blessé(e)

**inner tube** chambre f à air

**insect** insecte m

**insecticide** insecticide m

**inside** à l'intérieur (de), dedans

**insomnia** insomnie f

**instant coffee** Nescafé® m

**instead of** au lieu de

**insurance** assurance f

**intend to…** avoir l'intention de…

**intermission** entracte m

**international** international(e)

**international money order** mandat m international

**Internet** Internet m

**Internet café** café m Internet, cybercafé m **98**

**interval** entracte m

**invite** inviter

**iron** (n) fer m à repasser; (v) repasser

**island** île f

**it** ce; il, elle; le, la, lui (see grammar); **it's beautiful** c'est beau; **it's warm** il fait chaud

**Italian** (n) Italien m, Italienne f; (language) italien m; (adj) italien m, italienne f

**Italy** Italie f

**itchy: it's itchy** ça me démange

**item** article m

**J**

**jacket** veste f; (bomber jacket) blouson m

**January** janvier m

**Japan** Japon m

**Japanese** (n) Japonais(e) m,f; (language) japonais m; (adj) japonais(e)

**jetlag** décalage m horaire

**jeweller's** bijouterie f

**jewellery** bijoux mpl

**job** travail m, (informal) boulot m

**jogging** jogging m

**journey** voyage m

**jug** carafe f

**juice** jus m

**July** juillet m

**jumper** pull m

**June** juin m

**just: just before/a little** juste avant/un peu; **just one** un seul; **I've just arrived** je viens d'arriver; **just in case** au cas où

**K**

**kayak** kayak m

**keep** garder

**key** clé f **30**, **37**, **39**

**kidney** rein m; (food) rognon m

**kill** tuer

**kilometre** kilomètre m

**kind: what kind of …?** quel genre de … ?

**kiss** (n) bise f; (v) embrasser

**kitchen** cuisine f

**Kleenex®** Kleenex® m

**knee** genou m

**knickers** culotte f

**knife** couteau m

**knock down/over** renverser; **to get knocked down/over** se faire renverser

**know** connaître, savoir

**L**

**ladies' (toilet)** toilettes *fpl* pour femmes
**lake** lac *m*
**lamp** lampe *f*
**landmark** (point *m* de) repère *m*
**landscape** paysage *m*
**language** langue *f*
**laptop** (ordinateur *m*) portable *m*
**last** *(adj)* dernier *m*, dernière *f*; **last year** l'année dernière
**last** *(v)* durer
**late** tard; *(in arriving)* en retard **25, 63**
**late-night opening** nocturne *f*
**latte** café *m* crème
**laugh** rire
**launderette** laverie *f*
**lawyer** avocat *m*
**leaflet** prospectus *m*, dépliant *m*
**leak** fuite *f*
**learn** apprendre
**least: the least** le/la moins; **at least** au moins
**leave** partir; laisser
**left** *(adj)* gauche; *(n)* gauche *f*; **to the left (of)** à gauche (de)
**left-luggage office** consigne *f*
**leg** jambe *f*
**lend** prêter
**lens** objectif *m*
**lenses** lentilles *fpl*
**less** moins; **less than** moins que
**let** laisser
**letter** lettre *f*
**letterbox** boîte *f* aux lettres
**library** bibliothèque *f*
**lie down** se coucher, s'étendre
**life** vie *f*
**lift** ascenseur *m*
**light** *(adj)* léger *m*, légère *f*; **light blue** bleu clair
**light** *(n)* lumière *f*

**light** *(v)* allumer
**light bulb** ampoule *f*
**lighter** briquet *m*
**lighthouse** phare *m*
**like** *(adv)* comme
**like** *(v)* aimer, aimer bien **19**; **I'd like …** j'aimerais …
**lip** lèvre *f*
**listen** écouter; **to listen to somebody/something** écouter quelqu'un/quelque chose
**listings magazine** guide *m* des spectacles
**litre** litre *m*
**little** *(adj)* petit(e)
**little** *(adv)* peu de; **a little** un peu; **little by little** petit à petit
**live** habiter, vivre
**liver** foie *m*
**living** vivant(e)
**living room** salon *m*
**local time** heure *f* locale
**lock** serrure *f*; *(bolt)* verrou *m*
**lollipop** sucette *f*
**long** long *m*, longue *f*; **a long time** longtemps; **how long …?** combien de temps … ?; **how long have you been here?** depuis quand êtes-vous ici ?
**look** regarder; **to look tired** avoir l'air fatigué
**look after** surveiller, s'occuper de
**look at** regarder
**look for** chercher
**look like** ressembler à
**lorry** camion *m*
**lose** perdre **30, 113**; **to get lost** se perdre; **to be lost** être perdu **12**
**lot: a lot (of)** beaucoup (de)
**loud** fort(e)
**low** bas *m*, basse *f*
**low blood pressure** hypotension *f*
**low tide** marée *f* basse
**luck** chance *f*
**lucky: to be lucky** avoir de la chance

**luggage** bagages *mpl* **25**
**lukewarm** tiède
**lunch** déjeuner *m*; **to have lunch** déjeuner
**lung** poumon *m*
**Luxembourg** Luxembourg *m*
**luxury** *(n)* luxe *m*; *(adj)* de luxe

# M

**magazine** magazine *m*, revue *f*
**maiden name** nom *m* de jeune fille
**mail** courrier *m*; *(e-mail)* e-mail *m*
**main** principal(e)
**main course** plat *m* principal
**make** faire; *(manufacture)* fabriquer
**man** homme *m*
**manage** se débrouiller; **to manage to do something** arriver à faire quelque chose
**management** direction *f*
**many** beaucoup (de); **how many?** combien?; **how many times …?** combien de fois … ?
**map** plan *m* **12**, **27**, **63**, **69**
**March** mars *m*
**market** marché *m* **84**
**marina** port *m* de plaisance
**marriage** mariage *m*
**married** marié(e)
**mass** messe *f*
**masterpiece** chef-d'œuvre *m*
**match** *(for lighting fire)* allumette *f*; *(game)* match *m*
**material** tissu *m*
**matter: it doesn't matter** ça ne fait rien
**mattress** matelas *m*
**May** mai *m*
**maybe** peut-être
**me** me; moi; **me too** moi aussi *(see grammar)*
**meal** repas *m*
**mean** vouloir dire, signifier

**medicine** médicament *m*
**medium** moyen *m*, moyenne *f*; *(steak)* à point
**meet** rencontrer; *(by arrangement)* rejoindre **63**
**meeting** réunion *f*
**member** membre *mf*
**memory** souvenir *m*; **in memory of** en souvenir de
**men** hommes *mpl*
**menu** carte *f*; *(set menu)* menu *m*
**Merry Christmas!** joyeux Noël !
**message** message *m* **102**
**metre** mètre *m*
**microwave** micro-ondes *m*
**midday** midi *m*
**middle** milieu *m*; **in the middle (of)** au milieu (de)
**midnight** minuit *m*
**might: it might rain** il risque de pleuvoir
**mill** moulin *m*
**mind: I don't mind** ça m'est égal
**mine** le mien, la mienne, les miens/miennes *(see grammar)*
**mineral water** eau *f* minérale
**minister** ministre *mf*
**minute** minute *f*; **at the last minute** au dernier moment
**mirror** glace *f*
**Miss** Mademoiselle *f*
**miss** rater, manquer **25**; **I miss him** il me manque; **there are two … missing** il manque deux …
**mistake** erreur *f*, faute *f*; **to make a mistake** se tromper
**mobile phone** *(telephone m)* portable *m* **113**
**modern** moderne
**moisturizer** crème *f* hydratante
**moment** moment *m*; **at the moment** en ce moment; **for the moment** pour le moment; **just a moment!** un moment !

**monastery** monastère m
**Monday** lundi m
**money** argent m
**month** mois m
**monument** monument m
**mood: to be in a good/bad mood**
être de bonne/mauvaise humeur
**moon** lune f
**moped** Mobylette® f
**more** plus; **more than** plus que;
**much more, a lot more** beaucoup
plus; **there's no more room** il n'y a
plus de place; **there are no more ...**
il n'y a plus de ...
**morning** matin m
**morning-after pill** pilule f du
lendemain
**mosque** mosquée f
**mosquito** moustique m
**most: the most** le/la plus; **most
people** la plupart des gens; **to make
the most of** profiter de
**mother** mère f
**motorbike** moto f
**motorcycle** moto f
**motorway** autoroute f
**mountain** montagne f
**mountain bike** VTT m
**mouse** souris f
**mouth** bouche f
**moving** émouvant(e)
**Mr** Monsieur m
**Mrs** Madame f
**much: how much?** combien ? **82**;
**how much is it?, how much does it
cost?** combien ça coûte ?
**mug** tasse f
**muscle** muscle m
**museum** musée m
**music** musique f
**must** devoir; **it must be 5 o'clock**
il doit être 5 heures; **I must go** il faut
que j'y aille
**mustard** moutarde f

**my** mon, ma, mes (see grammar)
**myself** moi-même

# N

**nail** (on finger, toe) ongle m; (for
attaching) clou m
**naked** nu(e)
**name** nom m; **my name is ...** je
m'appelle ...
**nap** sieste f; **to have a nap** faire la
sieste
**napkin** serviette f (de table)
**nappy** couche f
**national holiday** fête f nationale
**nature** nature f
**near** près; proche; **near the beach** près
de la plage; **the nearest** le plus proche
**necessary** nécessaire
**neck** cou m
**need** avoir besoin de
**negative** négatif m
**neighbour** voisin(e) m,f
**neither: neither do I** moi non plus;
**neither ... nor ...** ni ... ni ...
**nephew** neveu m
**nervous** nerveux m, nerveuse f
**Netherlands** Pays-Bas mpl
**never** ne ... jamais
**new** nouveau m, nouvelle f; (brand new)
neuf m, neuve f
**news** nouvelles fpl
**newsagent** marchand m de journaux
**newspaper** journal m
**New Year** nouvel an m
**next** (adj) prochain(e), suivant(e); (adv)
ensuite
**nice** agréable; (informal) sympa
**niece** nièce f
**night** nuit f **35**, **38**
**nightclub** boîte f de nuit
**nightdress** chemise f de nuit
**no** non; aucun(e); **no, thank you** non
merci; **no idea** aucune idée

**nobody** personne
**noise** bruit *m*; **to make a noise** faire du bruit
**noisy** bruyant(e)
**none** aucun(e)
**non-smokers** non-fumeurs *mpl*
**noon** midi *m*
**north** nord *m*; **in the north** au nord; **(to the) north of** au nord de
**North Sea** mer *f* du Nord
**nose** nez *m*
**not** ne … pas; **not yet** pas encore; **not any** aucun(e); **not at all** pas du tout
**note** mot *m*
**notebook** cahier *m*
**nothing** ne … rien
**novel** roman *m*
**November** novembre *m*
**now** maintenant
**nowadays** de nos jours
**nowhere** nulle part
**number** numéro *m*; *(numeral)* nombre *m*
**nurse** infirmière *f*

## O

**obvious** évident(e)
**occupation** métier *m*
**ocean** océan *m*
**o'clock: one o'clock** une heure; **three o'clock** trois heures
**October** octobre *m*
**of** de
**offer** *(v)* offrir
**often** souvent
**oil** huile *f*
**ointment** pommade *f*
**OK** d'accord, *(informal)* ok
**old** vieux *m*, vieille *f*; *(former)* ancien *m*, ancienne *f*; **how old are you?** quel âge as-tu?; **old people** les personnes âgées *fpl*
**old town** vieille ville *f*
**on** sur; **it's on at …** ça joue à …

**once** une fois; **once a day/an hour** une fois par jour/heure
**one** *(number)* un; *(personal pronoun)* on
**only** ne … que, seulement
**open** *(adj)* ouvert(e); *(v)* ouvrir
**operate** opérer
**operation: to have an operation** se faire opérer
**opinion** avis *m*, opinion *f*; **in my opinion** à mon avis
**opportunity** occasion *f*
**opposite** *(adj)* contraire; *(prep)* en face de
**optician** opticien *m*
**or** ou
**orange** *(adj)* orange; *(n) (fruit)* orange *f*; *(colour)* orange *m*
**orchestra** orchestre *m*
**order** *(n)* commande *f*; *(v)* commander **45**
**organic** bio
**organize** organiser
**other** autre; **others** d'autres
**otherwise** sinon
**our** notre, nos *(see grammar)*
**ours** le/la nôtre, les nôtres *(see grammar)*
**out of order** hors service
**outside** dehors; *(in the open air)* en plein air
**outward journey** aller *n*
**oven** four *m*
**over** sur, au-dessus de; **over there** là-bas
**overdone** trop cuit(e)
**owe** devoir **48**
**own** *(adj)* propre; *(v)* posséder
**owner** propriétaire *mf*

## P

**pack:** *(v)* **to pack one's bags** faire ses valises
**package holiday** voyage *m* organisé

**packed** bondé(e)

**packet** paquet *m*

**painting** peinture *f*, tableau *m*

**pair** paire *f*; **a pair of pyjamas/shorts** un pyjama *m*/short *m*

**palace** palais *m*

**pants** *(woman's)* culotte *f*, *(man's)* slip *m*

**paper napkin** serviette *f* en papier

**parcel** colis *m*

**pardon?** comment ?

**parents** parents *mpl*

**park** *(n)* parc *m*; *(v)* se garer

**parking space** place *f* de parking

**part** partie *f*; **to be a part of** faire partie de

**party** *(for an occasion)* fête *f*; *(in the evening)* soirée *f*

**pass** *(n)* forfait *m*

**pass** *(v)* passer; **to be passing through** être de passage

**passenger** passager *m*, passagère *f*

**passport** passeport *m*

**past** passé *m*; **a quarter past ten** dix heures et quart

**path** chemin *m*, sentier *m* **76**

**patient** patient(e)

**pay** payer **83**

**pedestrian** piéton *m*, piétonne *f*

**pedestrian street** rue *f* piétonne

**pee: to have a pee** faire pipi

**peel** peler

**pen** stylo *m*

**pencil** crayon *m*

**people** (les) gens *mpl*

**percent** pour cent

**perfect** parfait(e)

**perfume** parfum *m*

**perhaps** peut-être

**periods** règles *fpl*

**person** personne *f*

**personal stereo** Walkman® *m*

**petrol** essence *f* **29**

**petrol station** station-service *f* **29**

**phone** *(n)* téléphone *m*; *(v)* téléphoner (à)

**phone box** cabine *f* téléphonique **101**

**phone call** coup *m* de téléphone; **to make a phone call** passer un coup de téléphone

**phonecard** carte *f* de téléphone **101**

**phone number** numéro *m* de téléphone

**photo** photo *f* **88, 89**; **to take a photo/photos** prendre une photo/des photos; **to take somebody's photo** prendre quelqu'un en photo

**photocopy** photocopie *f*; **to make a photocopy** faire une photocopie

**picnic** pique-nique *m*; **to have a picnic** pique-niquer

**piece** morceau *m*; **a piece of** un morceau de; **a piece of advice/fruit** un conseil/fruit

**piles** hémorroïdes *fpl*

**pill** pilule *f*; **to be on the pill** prendre la pilule

**pillow** oreiller *m*

**pillowcase** taie *f* d'oreiller

**PIN (number)** code *m* confidentiel

**pink** *(adj)* rose; *(n)* *(flower)* rose *f*; *(colour)* rose *m*

**pity: it's a pity** c'est dommage

**place** lieu *m*

**plan** *(v)* prévoir

**plane** avion *m* **25**

**plant** plante *f*

**plaster (cast)** plâtre *m*

**plastic** plastique *m*

**plastic bag** sac *m* plastique

**plate** assiette *f*

**platform** quai *m* **27**

**play** *(n)* pièce *f* de théâtre; *(v)* jouer (à)

**please** *(v)* plaire; *(adv)* *(informal)* s'il te plaît, *(polite or plural)* s'il vous plaît

**pleased** content(e); **pleased to meet you!** enchanté(e) !

**pleasure** plaisir *m*

**plug** prise *f*

**plug in** brancher

**plumber** plombier m
**point** point m
**police** police f
**policeman** policier m
**police station** commissariat m **113**
**poor** pauvre
**port** port m
**portrait** portrait m
**Portugal** Portugal m
**Portuguese** (n) Portugais(e) m,f; (language) portugais m; (adj) portugais(e)
**possible** possible
**post** poste f; (mail received) courrier m
**postbox** boîte f aux lettres **95**
**postcard** carte f postale
**postcode** code m postal
**poster** affiche f
**postman** facteur m
**post office** bureau m de poste **94**
**pot** pot m
**pound** livre f (sterling); (for cars) fourrière f
**powder** poudre f
**practical** pratique
**prefer** préférer
**pregnant** enceinte **109**
**prepare** préparer
**present** cadeau m
**press** appuyer
**pressure** pression f
**pretty** joli(e), mignon m, mignonne f
**previous** précédent(e)
**price** prix m, tarif m
**private** privé(e)
**prize** prix m
**probably** probablement
**problem** problème m
**product** produit m
**programme** émission f, programme m
**promise** promettre
**propose** proposer
**protect** protéger; **to protect oneself** se protéger

**proud** fier m, fière f
**public** public m
**public holiday** jour m férié
**pull** tirer
**purple** (adj) violet m, violette f; (n) violet m
**purpose: on purpose** exprès
**purse** porte-monnaie m
**push** pousser
**pushchair** poussette f
**put** mettre
**put out** éteindre
**put up** héberger
**put up with** supporter

## Q

**quality** qualité f; **of good/bad quality** de bonne/mauvaise qualité
**quarter** quart m; **a quarter of an hour** un quart d'heure; **a quarter to ten** dix heures moins le quart
**quay** quai m
**question** question f
**queue** (n) queue f; (v) faire la queue
**quick** rapide
**quickly** vite, rapidement
**quiet** calme, tranquille
**quite** assez de; **quite a lot of** pas mal de

## R

**racist** raciste
**racket** raquette f
**radiator** radiateur m
**radio** radio f
**radio station** station f de radio
**rain** (n) pluie f
**rain:** (v) **it's raining** il pleut
**raincoat** imperméable m
**random: at random** au hasard
**rape** viol m
**rare** rare; (meat) saignant(e)

**rarely** rarement
**rather** plutôt
**raw** cru(e)
**razor** rasoir m
**razor blade** lame f de rasoir
**reach** arriver à
**read** lire
**ready** prêt(e)
**reasonable** raisonnable
**receipt** reçu m, ticket m de caisse **83**
**receive** recevoir
**reception** accueil m, réception f; **at reception** à la réception **38**
**receptionist** réceptionniste mf
**recipe** recette f
**recognize** reconnaître
**recommend** recommander **43**
**record** (n) disque m; (v) enregistrer
**record dealer** disquaire m
**red** (adj) rouge; (hair) roux m, rousse f; (n) rouge m
**red light** feu m rouge
**reduce** diminuer
**reduction** réduction f
**red wine** vin m rouge
**refund** (n) remboursement m; **to get a refund** se faire rembourser
**refund** (v) rembourser
**refuse** refuser
**registered** en recommandé
**registration number** numéro m d'immatriculation
**remember** se souvenir (de)
**remind** rappeler; **that reminds me of ...** ça me rappelle ...
**remove** enlever
**rent** (n) loyer m; (v) louer **39**; **for rent** à louer
**rental** location f
**reopen** rouvrir
**repair** réparer **30**; **to get something repaired** faire réparer quelque chose
**repeat** répéter **10**
**reserve** réserver **44**

**reserved** réservé(e)
**rest:** (n) **the rest** le reste
**rest** (v) se reposer
**restaurant** restaurant m **43**
**return** retour m
**return ticket** aller-retour m
**reverse-charge call** appel m en PCV **101**
**reverse gear** marche f arrière
**review** critique f
**rheumatism** rhumatismes mpl
**rib** côte f
**right** (n) (entitlement) droit m; (side) droite f; **to have the right to ...** avoir le droit de ...; **to the right (of)** à droite (de)
**right** (adj) bon m, bonne f; **to be right** avoir raison
**right:** (adv) **right away** tout de suite; **right beside** tout près de
**ring** bague f
**ripe** mûr(e)
**rip-off** arnaque f
**risk** risque m
**river** fleuve m, rivière f
**road** route f; (street) rue f
**road sign** panneau m
**rock** rocher m
**rollerblades** rollers mpl
**room** pièce f, salle f; (bedroom) chambre f **35**, **36**
**rosé wine** rosé m
**round** tournée f
**roundabout** rond-point m
**rubbish** ordures fpl; **to take the rubbish out** sortir les poubelles
**rucksack** sac m à dos
**rug** tapis m
**ruins** ruines fpl; **in ruins** en ruines
**run out: to have run out of petrol** être en panne d'essence **30**

**sad** triste
**safe** en sécurité
**safety** sécurité f
**safety belt** ceinture f de sécurité
**sail** voile f
**sailing** voile f; **to go sailing** faire de la voile
**sailing boat** bateau m à voile
**sale: for sale** à vendre; **in the sale** en solde
**sales** soldes fpl
**salt** sel m
**salted** salé(e)
**salty** salé(e)
**same** même, pareil m, pareille f; **the same** le même m, la même f, les mêmes mfpl
**sand** sable m
**sandals** sandales fpl
**sanitary towel** serviette f hygiénique
**Saturday** samedi m
**saucepan** casserole f
**save** sauver; (on computer) sauvegarder; **to save time** gagner du temps
**say** dire; **how do you say ...?** comment dit-on ... ?
**scared: to be scared (of)** avoir peur (de)
**scenery** paysage m
**scissors** ciseaux mpl
**scoop** (of ice cream) boule f
**scooter** scooter m
**scotch** whisky m
**scuba diving** plongée f sous-marine
**sea** mer f
**seafood** fruits mpl de mer
**seasick: to be seasick** avoir le mal de mer
**seaside: at the seaside** au bord de la mer
**seaside resort** station f balnéaire
**season** saison f

**seat** place f 23
**sea view** vue f sur mer
**seaweed** algues fpl
**second** seconde f
**second class** deuxième classe f
**secondary school** collège m; (age 15-18) lycée m
**second-hand** d'occasion
**secure** en sécurité
**security** sécurité f
**see** voir; **see you later!** à plus tard !, à tout à l'heure !; **see you soon!** à bientôt !, à la prochaine !; **see you tomorrow!** à demain !
**seem** paraître; **it seems that ...** il paraît que ...
**seldom** pas souvent
**self-confidence** confiance f en soi
**sell** vendre
**Sellotape®** Scotch® m
**send** envoyer
**sender** expéditeur m
**sense** sens m
**sensitive** sensible
**sentence** phrase f
**separate** séparer
**separately** séparément
**September** septembre m
**serious** sérieux m, sérieuse f; (accident etc) grave
**several** plusieurs
**sex** sexe m
**shade** ombre f; **in the shade** à l'ombre
**shame** honte f
**shampoo** shampooing m
**shape** forme f
**share** partager
**shave** se raser
**shaving cream** crème f à raser
**shaving foam** mousse f à raser
**she** elle
**sheet** drap m; (of paper) feuille f
**shellfish** crustacés mpl

**shirt** chemise f
**shock** choc m
**shocking** choquant(e)
**shoes** chaussures fpl
**shop** magasin m
**shop assistant** vendeur m, vendeuse f
**shopkeeper** marchand(e) m,f
**shopping** courses fpl; (for clothes, presents) shopping m; **to do some/the shopping** faire des/les courses
**shopping centre** centre m commercial
**short** court(e); **I'm two … short** il me manque deux …
**short cut** raccourci m
**shorts** short m
**short-sleeved** en/à manches courtes
**shoulder** épaule f
**show** (n) spectacle m; (v) montrer
**shower** douche f; **to take a shower** prendre une douche
**shower gel** gel m douche
**shut** fermer
**shuttle** navette f
**shy** timide
**sick: to feel sick** avoir mal au cœur
**side** côté m
**sign** (n) panneau m; (v) signer
**sign up** s'inscrire
**signal** réception f
**silver** argent m
**since** depuis (que); (because) puisque
**sing** chanter
**singer** chanteur m, chanteuse f
**single** célibataire mf
**single (ticket)** aller m (simple)
**sister** sœur f
**sit down** s'asseoir
**size** taille f; (of shoes) pointure f
**ski** ski m
**ski boots** chaussures fpl de ski
**skiing** ski m; **to go skiing** faire du ski
**ski lift** remontée f mécanique
**ski pole** bâton m de ski
**ski resort** station f de ski

**skin** peau f
**skirt** jupe f
**sky** ciel m
**skyscraper** gratte-ciel m
**sleep** (n) sommeil m
**sleep** (v) dormir; **to sleep with** coucher avec
**sleeping bag** sac m de couchage
**sleeping pill** somnifère m
**sleepy: to be sleepy** avoir sommeil
**sleeve** manche f
**slice** tranche f
**sliced** coupé(e) en tranches
**slide** diapositive f
**slow** lent(e)
**slowly** lentement, doucement
**small** petit(e); **smaller than** plus petit(e) que
**smell** (n) odeur f
**smell** (v) sentir; **to smell good/bad** sentir bon/mauvais
**smile** (n) sourire m; (v) sourire
**smoke** fumer
**smoker** fumeur m, fumeuse f
**snack** casse-croûte m
**snow** (n) neige f; (v) neiger
**so** si, alors; **so that** pour que
**soap** savon m
**soccer** football m
**society** société f
**socks** chaussettes fpl
**some** (adj) quelques; (pron) quelques-uns mpl, quelques-unes fpl
**somebody, someone** quelqu'un
**something** quelque chose; **something else** autre chose
**sometimes** quelquefois
**somewhere** quelque part; **somewhere else** ailleurs
**son** fils m
**song** chanson f
**soon** bientôt
**sore: to have a sore throat/head** avoir mal à la gorge/tête

**sorry** désolé(e); **sorry!** pardon !
**south** sud *m*; **in the south** au sud; **(to the) south of** au sud de
**souvenir** souvenir *m*
**Spain** Espagne *f*
**Spanish** *(n)* Espagnol(e) *m,f; (language)* espagnol *m; (adj)* espagnol(e)
**spare ...** ... de rechange
**spare part** pièce *f* de rechange
**spare wheel** roue *f* de secours
**sparkling water** eau *f* gazeuse
**speak** parler **8, 10, 102, 113**
**special** spécial(e); **it's nothing special** ça n'a rien d'exceptionnel; **today's special** plat *m* du jour **45**
**speciality** spécialité *f*
**speed** vitesse *f*; **at full speed** à toute vitesse
**spell** épeler **10**
**spend** dépenser; *(time)* passer
**spice** épice *f*
**spicy** épicé(e)
**spider** araignée *f*
**splinter** écharde *f*
**split up** se séparer
**spoil** gâter
**sponge** éponge *f*
**spoon** cuillère *f*
**sport** sport *m*
**sports ground** terrain *m* de sport
**sporty** sportif *m*, sportive *f*
**spot** *(place)* emplacement *m; (pimple)* bouton *m*; **on the spot** sur place
**sprain: to sprain one's ankle** se fouler la cheville
**spring** printemps *m*
**square** place *f*
**stadium** stade *m*
**stain** tache *f*
**stained-glass windows** vitraux *mpl*
**stairs** escalier *m*
**stamp** timbre *m* **95**
**stand** *(n)* stand *m*
**start** commencer

**state** état *m*
**statement** déclaration *f*
**station** gare *f*
**stay** *(n)* séjour *m*
**stay** *(v)* rester; **to stay in touch** rester en contact
**steal** voler **113**
**step** marche *f*
**sticking plaster** sparadrap *m*
**still** encore, toujours
**still water** eau *f* plate
**sting** *(n)* piqûre *f*
**sting** *(v)* piquer; **to get stung (by)** se faire piquer (par)
**stock: out of stock** épuisé(e)
**stomach** estomac *m; (belly)* ventre *m*
**stone** pierre *f*
**stop** *(n)* arrêt *m* **28**; *(v)* arrêter, s'arrêter
**stopcock** robinet *m* d'arrêt
**storm** orage *m*, tempête *f*
**story** histoire *f*
**straight ahead, straight on** tout droit
**strange** bizarre
**street** rue *f*
**strong** fort(e)
**stuck** bloqué(e), coincé(e)
**student** étudiant(e) *m,f* **15, 23**
**studies** études *fpl*
**study** étudier; **to study biology** faire des études de biologie
**style** style *m*
**subtitled** sous-titré(e)
**suburb(s)** banlieue *f*
**suffer** souffrir
**suggest** proposer
**suit: does that suit you?** ça vous va ?; **that suits you** ça vous va bien
**suitcase** valise *f* **25**
**summer** été *m*
**sun** soleil *m*; **in the sun** au soleil
**sunbathe** bronzer
**sunburnt: to get sunburnt** prendre un coup de soleil

**sun cream** crème f solaire
**Sunday** dimanche m
**sunglasses** lunettes fpl de soleil
**sunhat** chapeau m de soleil
**sunrise** lever m du soleil
**sunset** coucher du soleil
**sunstroke** insolation f; **to get
  sunstroke** attraper une insolation
**supermarket** supermarché m **39**, **82**
**supplement** supplément m
**sure** sûr(e); *(yes)* bien sûr
**surf** surfer
**surfboard** planche f de surf
**surfing** surf m; **to go surfing** faire
  du surf
**surgical spirit** alcool m à 90°
**surname** nom m de famille
**surprise** *(n)* surprise f; *(v)* étonner
**sweat** transpirer
**sweater** pull m
**sweet** *(n)* bonbon m; *(adj)* sucré(e)
**swim:** *(n)* **to go for a swim** se baigner
**swim** *(v)* nager
**swimming** natation f
**swimming pool** piscine f
**swimming trunks** slip m de bain
**swimsuit** maillot m de bain
**switchboard operator** standardiste mf
**switch off** éteindre
**switch on** allumer
**swollen** enflé(e)
**syrup** sirop m

# T

**table** table f **44**
**tablespoon** cuillère f à soupe
**tablet** comprimé m
**take** prendre; *(to/from a place)*
  emmener, emporter; **it takes 2 hours**
  ça prend 2 heures
**takeaway** à emporter
**take off** *(plane)* décoller
**talk** parler

**tall** grand(e)
**tampon** tampon m
**tan** bronzer
**tanned** bronzé(e)
**tap** robinet m
**taste** *(n)* goût m; *(v)* goûter
**tax** taxe f
**tax-free** hors taxes
**taxi** taxi m **31**
**taxi driver** chauffeur m de taxi
**T-bar** tire-fesses m
**team** équipe f
**teaspoon** cuillère f à café
**teenager** adolescent(e) m,f
**telephone** *(n)* téléphone m; *(v)*
  téléphoner (à)
**telephone directory** annuaire m
**television** télévision f
**tell** raconter
**tell off** engueuler
**temperature** température f; **to have
  a temperature** avoir de la fièvre; **to
  take one's temperature** prendre sa
  température
**temple** temple m
**temporary** temporaire
**tennis** tennis m
**tennis court** court m de tennis
**tennis shoes** tennis fpl
**tent** tente f
**tent peg** sardine f
**terminal** terminal m
**terrace** terrasse f
**terrible** terrible
**text message** SMS m
**thank** remercier; **thank you** merci;
  **thank you very much** merci
  beaucoup
**thanks** merci; **thanks to** grâce à
**that** cela, ça; *ce* m, *cette* f; que; **that
  one** celui-là m, celle-là f
**the** le, la, les *(see grammar)*
**theatre** théâtre m
**theft** vol m

**their** leur, leurs *(see grammar)*
**theirs** le/la leur, les leurs *(see grammar)*
**them** les; eux; leur *(see grammar)*
**theme park** parc m d'attractions
**then** alors, ensuite
**there** y, là; **there is** il y a; **there are** il y a; **there is a castle** il y a un château; **there are two museums** il y a deux musées
**therefore** donc
**thermometer** thermomètre m
**Thermos® flask** thermos® m
**these** ces; **these ones** ceux-ci m, celles-ci f
**they** ils, elles; les *(see grammar)* **they say that …** on dit que …
**thief** voleur m, voleuse f
**thigh** cuisse f
**thin** maigre
**thing** chose f; **things** affaires fpl
**think** penser, croire, réfléchir
**think about** penser à
**thirst** soif f
**thirsty: to be thirsty** avoir soif
**this** cela, ça; ce m, cette f; **this one** celui-ci m, celle-ci f; **this evening** ce soir; **this is …** je te présente …
**those** ces; **those ones** ceux-là m, celles-là f
**throat** gorge f
**throw** jeter
**throw out** jeter, mettre à la poubelle
**Thursday** jeudi m
**ticket** *(for train, plane, show)* billet m **23**, **64**; *(for bus, underground)* ticket m
**ticket office** billetterie f
**tidy** ranger
**tie** cravate f
**tight** serré(e)
**tights** collant(s) mpl
**time** temps m **120**; fois f; **what time is it?** quelle heure est-il ?; **from time to time** de temps en temps; **to have (the) time to …** avoir le temps de

…; **on time** à l'heure; **three/four times** trois/quatre fois
**time difference** décalage m horaire
**timetable** horaires mpl **23**
**tinfoil** papier m alu
**tip** pourboire m
**tired** fatigué(e)
**tobacco** tabac m
**tobacconist's** bureau m de tabac
**today** aujourd'hui
**together** ensemble
**toilet** toilettes fpl, WC mpl **8**
**toilet bag** trousse f de toilette
**toilet paper** papier m toilette
**toiletries** affaires fpl de toilette
**toll** péage m
**tomorrow** demain; **tomorrow evening** demain soir
**tongue** langue f
**tonight** ce soir
**too** aussi; trop; **too bad** tant pis; **too many** trop de; **too much** trop de
**tooth** dent f
**toothbrush** brosse f à dents
**toothpaste** dentifrice m
**top** haut m; **at the top** en haut
**torch** lampe f de poche
**touch** toucher
**tourist** touriste mf
**tourist office** office m de tourisme
**tourist trap** attrape-touristes m
**towards** vers
**towel** serviette f; **bath/beach towel** serviette f de bain/de plage
**town** ville f
**town centre** centre-ville m
**town hall** mairie f, hôtel m de ville
**toy** jouet m
**traditional** traditionnel m, traditionnelle f, folklorique
**traffic** circulation f
**traffic jam** bouchon m, embouteillage m **29**
**trailer** bande-annonce f

**train** train *m* **27**; **the train to Avignon** le train en direction d'Avignon
**train station** gare *f*
**tram** tramway *m*
**transfer** *(of money)* virement *m*
**translate** traduire
**travel** voyager; **to travel alone** voyager seul
**travel agency** agence *f* de voyages
**traveller's cheque** Traveller's Cheque® *m*, chèque *m* de voyage
**trip** voyage *m*; excursion *f*; **have a good trip!** bon voyage !
**trolley** Caddie® *m*, chariot *m*
**trouble: to have trouble doing something** avoir du mal à faire quelque chose
**trousers** pantalon *m*
**true** vrai(e)
**try** essayer **85**; **to try to do something** essayer de faire quelque chose
**try on** essayer
**tube** métro *m*
**tube station** station *f* de métro
**Tuesday** mardi *m*
**tupperware** tupperware *m*
**turn:** *(n)* **it's your turn** c'est ton tour
**turn** *(v)* tourner
**twice** deux fois
**type** *(n)* type *m*; *(v)* taper
**typical** typique
**tyre** pneu *m*

# U

**umbrella** parapluie *m*
**uncle** oncle *m*
**uncomfortable** pas à l'aise
**under** sous
**underground** métro *m*
**underground line** ligne *f* de métro
**underground station** station *f* de métro
**underneath** dessous

**understand** comprendre **10**
**underwear** sous-vêtements *mpl*
**United Kingdom** Royaume-Uni *m*
**United States** États-Unis *mpl*
**until** jusqu'à
**upset** *(distressed)* affecté(e); *(annoyed)* contrarié(e); *(offended)* vexé(e)
**upstairs** en haut, là-haut
**urgent** urgent(e)
**us** nous
**use** se servir de, utiliser; **to be used for** servir à; **I'm used to it** j'ai l'habitude; **I'm not used to eating so early** je n'ai pas l'habitude de manger aussi tôt
**useful** utile
**useless** inutile
**usually** d'habitude
**U-turn** demi-tour *m*

# V

**vaccinated (against)** vacciné(e) (contre)
**valid** en cours de validité; **valid (for)** valable (pour)
**valley** vallée *f*
**VAT** TVA *f*
**vegetarian** végétarien *m*, végétarienne *f*
**very** très
**view** vue *f*
**village** village *m*
**visa** visa *m*
**visit** *(n)* visite *f*; *(v) (place)* visiter; *(person)* rendre visite à
**volleyball** volley(-ball) *m*
**vomit** vomir

# W

**waist** taille *f*
**wait** attendre; **to wait for somebody/something** attendre quelqu'un/quelque chose

**waiter** serveur *m*

**waitress** serveuse *f*

**wake up** (se) réveiller

**walk:** *(n)* **to go for a walk** aller se promener, se balader

**walk** *(v)* marcher; *(go for a walk)* se promener

**walking: to go walking** faire de la marche

**walking boots** chaussures *fpl* de marche

**Walkman®** Walkman® *m*

**wallet** portefeuille *m*

**want** vouloir; **to want to do something** avoir envie de faire quelque chose

**warm** chaud(e); *(welcome etc)* chaleureux *m*, chaleureuse *f*

**warn** prévenir

**wash:** *(n)* **to have a wash** se laver

**wash** *(v)* laver; **to wash one's hair** se laver les cheveux

**washbasin** lavabo *m*

**washing: to do the washing** faire la lessive

**washing machine** machine *f* à laver

**washing powder** lessive *f*

**washing-up liquid** liquide *m* vaisselle

**wasp** guêpe *f*

**waste** gâcher; **to waste time** perdre du temps

**watch** *(n)* montre *f*

**watch** *(v)* regarder; **watch out!** attention!

**water** eau *f* **45**

**water heater** chauffe-eau *m*

**waterproof** imperméable *m*

**waterproof jacket** K-way® *m*

**waterskiing** ski *m* nautique

**wave** vague *f*

**way** *(route)* chemin *m*; *(manner)* façon *f*, manière *f*

**way in** entrée *f*

**way out** sortie *f*

**we** nous

**weak** faible

**wear** porter

**weather** temps *m* **21**; **the weather's bad** il fait mauvais

**weather forecast** prévisions *fpl* météo **21**

**website** site *m* Internet

**Wednesday** mercredi *m*

**week** semaine *f*

**weekend** week-end *m*

**welcome** bienvenu(e); **welcome!** bienvenue !; **you're welcome** il n'y a pas de quoi

**well** bien; **I'm very well** je vais bien; **well done** bien cuit; **well done!** bravo !

**well-known** connu(e)

**west** ouest *m*; **in the west** à l'ouest; **(to the) west of** à l'ouest de

**wet** mouillé(e)

**wetsuit** combinaison *f* de plongée

**what** qu'est-ce que, quoi; **what do you want?** que veux-tu ?; **what I liked most** ce que j'ai le plus aimé

**wheel** roue *f*

**wheelchair** fauteuil *m* roulant

**when** quand

**where** où; **where is/are …?** où est/ sont … ?; **where are you from?** d'où viens-tu ?; **where are you going?** où vas-tu ?

**which** quel *m*, quelle *f*

**while** pendant que

**whisky** whisky *m*

**white** *(adj)* blanc *m*, blanche *f*; *(n)* blanc *m*

**who** qui; **who's calling?** qui est à l'appareil ?

**whole** entier *m*, entière *f*; **the whole cake** le gâteau en entier

**whose** dont

**why** pourquoi

**wide** large

**wife** femme *f*

**wild** sauvage

**wind** vent *m*

**window** fenêtre *f*, vitre *f*; **in the window** en vitrine **85**

**windscreen** pare-brise *m*

**windsurfing** planche *f* à voile

**wine** vin *m* **45**

**winter** hiver *m*

**with** avec

**withdraw** retirer

**without** sans

**woman** femme *f*

**wonderful** formidable

**wood** bois *m*

**wool** laine *f*

**work** *(n)* travail *m*

**work** *(v)* travailler; *(function)* marcher; **to work in** travailler dans

**work of art** œuvre *f* d'art

**works** travaux *mpl*

**world** monde *m*

**worry** *(n)* souci *m*; *(v)* s'inquiéter

**worse** pire; **to get worse** s'aggraver; **it's worse (than)** c'est pire (que)

**worth: to be worth** valoir; **it's worth it** ça vaut la peine; **it's worth …** ça vaut …

**wound** plaie *f*

**wrist** poignet *m*

**write** écrire **10**, **83**

**wrong** faux *m*, fausse *f*; **to be wrong** avoir tort

## XYZ

**X-rays** rayons X *mpl*

**year** an *m*, année *f*

**yellow** *(adj)* jaune; *(n)* jaune *m*

**yes** oui

**yesterday** hier; **yesterday evening** hier soir

**you** tu, vous; te, vous; toi, vous *(see grammar)*

**young** jeune

**your** ton, ta, tes, votre, vos *(see grammar)*

**yours** le tien, la tienne, les tiens/tiennes, le/la vôtre, les vôtres *(see grammar)*

**youth hostel** auberge *f* de jeunesse

**zero** zéro *m*

**zip** fermeture *f* Éclair®

**zoo** zoo *m*

**zoom (lens)** zoom *m*

# DICTIONARY

## FRENCH-ENGLISH

### A

**à: aller à Paris/à la gare** to go to Paris/to the station; **être à Paris** to be in Paris; **à 2 km** 2 km away; **à 3 heures** at 3 o'clock
**abbaye** abbey
**abeille** bee
**abîmé** damaged
**abord: d'abord** first (of all)
**abordable** affordable
**accepter** to accept
**accès** access
**accident** accident
**accompagner** to go with; to come with; to take
**accord: d'accord** OK; **je suis d'accord** I agree
**accueil** reception; information
**accueillant** welcoming
**acheter** to buy
**adaptateur** adaptor
**addition** bill
**adolescent** teenager
**adorer** to love
**adresse** address
**adresse électronique** e-mail address
**adulte** adult
**aéroport** airport
**affaires** business; things; **pour affaires** on business
**affiche** poster
**Afrique** Africa
**âge** age; **quel âge as-tu ?** how old are you?
**agence de voyages** travel agency

**aggraver: s'aggraver** to get worse
**agréable** nice
**agresser** to attack
**aide** help
**aider** to help
**ailleurs** somewhere else; **d'ailleurs** anyway
**aimer** to like; to love; **j'aimerais …** I'd like …
**air** air; **en plein air** outside; **avoir l'air …** to look …
**aise: à l'aise** comfortable; **pas à l'aise** uncomfortable
**alcool** alcohol
**alcool à 90°** surgical spirit
**algues** seaweed
**Allemagne** Germany
**Allemand** German
**aller** (n) outward journey; **un aller (simple)** a single (ticket)
**aller** (v) to go; **s'en aller** to go (away); **comment allez-vous ?** how are you?; **je vais bien** I'm very well; **ça va ?** how are you?; **ça va** I'm fine; **ça vous va ?** does that suit you?; **ça vous va bien** that suits you
**allergique** allergic
**aller-retour** return (ticket)
**allô** hello
**allumer** to light; to switch on
**allumette** match
**alors** so; then
**ambassade** embassy
**ambiance** atmosphere
**ambulance** ambulance
**amende** fine

**amener** to bring
**américain** American
**ami(e)** friend; **petit ami** boyfriend; **petite amie** girlfriend
**amour** love
**amoureux: être amoureux (de)** to be in love (with); **tomber amoureux (de)** to fall in love (with)
**ampoule** (light) bulb; blister
**amusant** funny
**amuser: s'amuser** to enjoy oneself
**an** year; **j'ai 22 ans** I'm 22 (years old)
**ancien** old; former
**anesthésie** anaesthetic
**angine** sore throat
**anglais** English, British
**Angleterre** England
**animal domestique** pet
**animé** busy
**année** year; **bonne année !** Happy New Year!
**anniversaire** birthday; anniversary; **bon anniversaire !** happy birthday!
**anniversaire de mariage** wedding anniversary
**annuaire** phone book
**annulé** cancelled
**annuler** to cancel
**antibiotique** antibiotic
**antiquité** antique
**août** August
**apéritif** aperitif; **prendre l'apéritif** to have a drink before lunch/dinner
**appareil: qui est à l'appareil ?** who's calling?
**appareil photo** camera
**appartement** flat
**appel** call
**appeler** to call; **s'appeler** to be called; **je m'appelle ...** my name is ...
**appendicite** appendicitis
**appétit: bon appétit !** enjoy your meal!
**apporter** to bring

**apprendre** to learn; to hear
**après** after
**après-demain** the day after tomorrow
**après-midi** afternoon
**appuyer** to press; **appuyer sur quelque chose** to press something
**araignée** spider
**argent** money; silver
**arnaque** rip-off
**arrêt** stop; **sans arrêt** continuously
**arrêt de bus** bus stop
**arrêter** to stop; **s'arrêter** to stop
**arrivée** arrival
**arriver** to arrive; to happen; **arriver à** to manage to; to reach
**art** art
**artisanal** traditionally made
**article** article; item
**artisan** craftsman
**artiste** artist
**ascenseur** lift
**Asie** Asia
**aspirine** aspirin
**asseoir: s'asseoir** to sit down
**assez** enough; quite; **assez de** enough
**assiette** plate
**assurance** insurance
**assurance tous risques** comprehensive insurance
**asthme** asthma
**attendre** to wait; **attendre quelqu'un/quelque chose** to wait for somebody/something
**attention: faire attention** to be careful; **attention !** watch out!, be careful!
**attrape-touristes** tourist trap
**auberge de jeunesse** youth hostel
**aucun(e)** *(adj)* no, not any; **aucune idée** no idea
**aucun** *(pron)* none
**aujourd'hui** today
**aussi** too, also; **moi aussi** me too; **aussi bien que** as well as

**auteur** author
**autobus** bus
**autocar** coach
**automne** autumn
**autoroute** motorway
**autre** other; **un(e) autre** another; **d'autres** others; **autre chose** something else
**avance: à l'avance** in advance; **en avance** early
**avant** before; **avant de faire** before doing
**avant-hier** the day before yesterday
**avec** with
**avenue** avenue
**aveugle** blind
**avion** plane; **par avion** airmail
**avis** opinion; **changer d'avis** to change one's mind
**avoir** to have
**avril** April

---

## B

**bagages** luggage, baggage
**bagages à main** hand luggage
**baigner: se baigner** to go for a swim
**bain** bath; **prendre un bain** to have a bath
**balader: se balader** to go for a walk; to go for a drive
**balcon** balcony
**balle** ball
**ballon** ball
**banlieue** suburb(s)
**banque** bank
**baptême** christening
**bas** *(n)* bottom; **en bas** at the bottom; downstairs
**bas** *(adj)* low
**basilique** basilica
**baskets** trainers
**basse** low
**bateau** boat

**bâtiment** building
**bâton** stick
**bâton de ski** ski pole
**batterie** battery
**bavarder** to chat
**beau** beautiful; handsome
**beaucoup (de)** a lot (of), many; **beaucoup plus** much more, a lot more
**bébé** baby
**belge** Belgian
**Belgique** Belgium
**belle** beautiful
**besoin: avoir besoin de** to need
**beurre** butter
**biberon** (baby's) bottle
**bibliothèque** library
**bicyclette** bicycle
**bien** *(adv)* well; *(adj)* good; **j'aimerais bien …** I'd (really) like …
**bien sûr** of course
**bientôt** soon; **à bientôt !** see you soon!
**bienvenu** welcome; **bienvenue !** welcome!
**bière** beer
**bijouterie** jeweller's
**bijoux** jewellery
**billet** ticket; (bank)note
**billetterie** ticket office
**bio** organic
**bise** kiss; **faire la bise à quelqu'un** to kiss somebody on both cheeks
**blanc** white
**blanche** white
**blessé** injured
**bleu** blue; bruise; *(steak)* very rare
**blond** blond
**bloqué** stuck
**blouson** jacket
**boire** to drink
**bois** wood
**boisson** drink
**boîte** box

**boîte aux lettres** letterbox; postbox
**boîte de conserve** can
**boîte de nuit** (night)club
**boîte de vitesses** gearbox
**bol** bowl
**bon** good; right; **bon marché** cheap
**bondé** packed
**bonjour** hello; good morning; good afternoon
**bonne** good
**bonsoir** hello; good evening
**bord: au bord de la mer** at the seaside
**bosse** bump
**bottes** boots
**bouche** mouth
**boucherie** butcher's
**bouchon** cork; traffic jam
**boucles d'oreilles** earrings
**bouée** buoy
**bougie** candle; spark plug
**boulangerie** baker's
**boule** bowl; scoop
**boules** bowls
**boules Quiès®** earplugs
**bout: un bout de …** a bit of …; **au bout de deux heures** after two hours; **au bout de la rue** at the end of the street
**bouteille** bottle
**bouteille de gaz** gas cylinder
**boutique** shop
**bouton** button; spot
**bracelet** bracelet
**branché** trendy
**brancher** to plug in
**bras** arm
**briquet** lighter
**bronchite** bronchitis
**bronzé** tanned
**bronzer** to tan; to sunbathe
**brosse** brush; hairbrush
**brosse à dents** toothbrush
**brouillard** fog

**bruit** noise; **faire du bruit** to make a noise
**brûler** to burn; **se brûler** to burn oneself
**brûlure** burn
**brun** brown
**bruyant** noisy
**bureau de poste** post office
**bureau de tabac** tobacconist's
**bus** bus
**but** goal; aim

# C

**ça** that; this; it
**cabine d'essayage** changing room
**cabine téléphonique** phone box
**cadeau** present
**Caddie®** trolley
**cafard** cockroach
**café** (black) coffee; café
**café au lait** white coffee
**café crème** white coffee, latte
**café Internet** Internet café
**cahier** notebook
**caisse** box; cashdesk, checkout
**caleçon** boxer shorts; swimming trunks
**calme** quiet
**caméra** camera
**camion** lorry
**campagne** country(side)
**camping** camping; campsite; **faire du camping** to go camping
**camping-car** camper
**camping-gaz®** camping stove
**capitale** capital
**car** coach
**carafe** jug
**caravane** caravan
**cardiaque** cardiac
**carie: avoir une carie** to have a cavity
**carnet de tickets** book of tickets
**carte** menu; map; card; **jouer aux cartes** to play cards

**Carte Bleue®** debit card
**carte de crédit** credit card
**carte de téléphone** phonecard
**carte d'identité** identity card
**carte postale** postcard
**cas: au cas où** just in case; **au cas où ...** in case ...; **en cas de ...** in case of ...
**casque** helmet
**casquette** cap
**cassé** broken
**casse-croûte** snack
**casser** to break; to split up; **se casser la jambe** to break one's leg
**casserole** (sauce)pan
**catastrophe** disaster
**cathédrale** cathedral
**catholique** (Roman) Catholic
**cause: à cause de** because of
**caution** deposit
**ce** this; that
**ceinture** belt
**ceinture de sécurité** seatbelt
**cela** that
**célèbre** famous
**celle-ci** this one
**celle-là** that one
**celui-ci** this one
**celui-là** that one
**cendrier** ashtray
**centime d'euro** euro cent
**centimètre** centimetre
**centre** centre
**centre commercial** shopping centre
**centre-ville** town centre
**certain** certain
**ces** these; those
**c'est** it's; **c'est très bon** it's very good; **c'est annulé** it's been cancelled
**cette** this; that
**ceux-ci** these ones
**ceux-là** those ones
**chacun** each one
**chaîne** chain; hi-fi; (TV) channel

**chaise** chair
**chaleur** heat
**chaleureux** warm
**chambre** room
**chambre à air** inner tube
**chambres d'hôte** bed and breakfast
**chance** luck; **bonne chance !** good luck!; **avoir de la chance** to be lucky
**changement** change
**changer** to change; **se changer** to get changed, to change
**chapeau** hat
**chapeau de soleil** sunhat
**chapelle** chapel
**chaque** each, every
**charcuterie** pork butcher's; cooked/cured meats
**chariot** trolley
**chasse d'eau** flush
**château** castle
**chaud** hot; **il fait chaud** it's hot; **boissons chaudes** hot drinks
**chauffage** heating
**chauffe-eau** water heater
**chauffeur de taxi** taxi driver
**chaussettes** socks
**chaussures** shoes
**chaussures de marche** walking boots
**chaussures de ski** ski boots
**chef** boss
**chemin** path; way
**cheminée** fireplace; chimney
**chemise** shirt
**chemise de nuit** nightdress
**chèque** cheque
**chèque de voyage** traveller's cheque
**cher** expensive; dear
**chercher** to look for; **aller chercher quelqu'un/quelque chose** to go and fetch somebody/something
**cheval** horse
**cheveux** hair
**cheville** ankle

**chez: chez lui** at/to his house; **je rentre chez moi** I'm going home
**chinois** Chinese
**choc** shock
**choisir** to choose
**choix** choice
**choquant** shocking
**chose** thing
**ciel** sky
**cigare** cigar
**cigarette** cigarette
**cimetière** cemetery
**cinéma** cinema
**cintre** coathanger
**circulation** traffic; circulation
**cirque** circus
**ciseaux** scissors
**clair** light; **bleu clair** light blue
**classe** class; **première/deuxième classe** first/second class
**classique** classic; classical
**clé** key
**clignotant** indicator
**climat** climate
**climatisation** air conditioning
**cochon** pig
**code** code
**code confidentiel** PIN (number)
**code d'entrée** door code
**code postal** postcode
**cœur** heart
**coffre** boot; chest
**coiffeur** hairdresser
**coin** corner; **un coin magnifique** a beautiful spot; **dans le coin** around here, in the area
**coincé** stuck
**colère: en colère** angry
**colis** parcel
**collant(s)** tights
**colle** glue
**colline** hill
**colonie** colony
**colonie de vacances** holiday camp

**combien** how many/much?; **combien ça coûte ?** how much is it?; **combien de temps … ?** how long …?; **depuis combien de temps … ?** for how long …?; **on est le combien ?** what's today's date?
**combinaison de plongée** wetsuit
**commander** to order
**comme** like, as
**commencer** to start, to begin
**comment** how; **comment ?** pardon?
**commerces** shops
**commissariat** (central) police station
**communiquer** to communicate
**compagnie aérienne** airline
**compartiment** compartment
**complet** whole; full; wholemeal
**comprendre** to understand
**comprimé** tablet
**compris** included; **tout compris** all inclusive
**comptant: payer comptant** to pay cash
**compte** account
**compte bancaire** bank account
**compter** to count
**compteur électrique** electricity meter
**concert** concert
**conduire** to drive; to take
**confirmer** to confirm
**confortable** comfortable
**congélateur** freezer
**connaître** to know
**connu** well-known
**conseil: un conseil** a piece of advice; **des conseils** advice; **demander conseil à quelqu'un** to ask somebody's advice
**conseiller** to advise
**consigne** left-luggage office
**consommer** to drink
**consommation** drink
**constipé** constipated
**consulat** consulate
**contact** contact; **rester en contact** to stay in touch

**contacter** to contact
**contagieux** contagious
**contemporain** contemporary
**content** pleased
**continuer** to continue, to go on;
  **continuer à faire quelque chose** to
  carry on doing something
**continuation: bonne continuation !**
  all the best!
**contraceptif** contraceptive
**contraire** opposite; **au contraire** on
  the contrary
**contrat** contract
**contre** against
**coordonnées** address and telephone
  number
**copain** friend; **petit copain** boyfriend
**copine** friend; **petite copine** girlfriend
**corbeille** basket
**corps** body
**correspondance** connection
**côté** side; **à côté de** beside
**côte** coast; rib; chop
**coton** cotton; cotton wool
**coton-tige®** cotton bud
**cou** neck
**couche** nappy
**coucher: se coucher** to go to bed; to
  lie down; **coucher avec** to sleep with
**coucher du soleil** sunset
**couette** quilt, duvet
**couleur** colour
**coup: ça vaut le coup** it's worth it;
  **aller boire un coup** to go for a drink
**coup de soleil: prendre un coup de
  soleil** to get sunburnt
**coupe-ongles** nail clippers
**couper** to cut; **se couper** to cut
  oneself; **coupé en tranches** sliced
**courage** courage; **bon courage !**
  good luck!
**courant: être au courant (de)** to
  know (about)
**courrier** mail, post

**cours** class, course
**courses** shopping; **faire des/les
  courses** to do some/the shopping
**court** short
**cousin** cousin
**couteau** knife
**coûter** to cost; **combien ça coûte ?**
  how much is it?
**couverture** blanket; cover
**couvrir** to cover
**cravate** tie
**crayon** pencil
**crème** cream
**crème à raser** shaving cream
**crème hydratante** moisturizer
**crème solaire** sun cream
**crevé** burst; exhausted
**crise cardiaque** heart attack
**crise d'appendicite** appendicitis
**croire** to believe; to think
**croisière** cruise
**cru** raw
**cuillère** spoon
**cuillère à café** teaspoon
**cuillère à soupe** tablespoon
**cuire** to cook; to bake
**cuisine** cooking; kitchen; **faire la
  cuisine** to do the cooking
**cuisinier** cook
**cuisinière** cooker; cook
**cuisse** thigh
**cuit** cooked; **bien cuit** well done; **trop
  cuit** overdone
**culotte** pants, knickers
**culte** (Protestant) church service
**cybercafé** Internet café

# D

**dangereux** dangerous
**dans** in; **dans une heure** in an hour;
  **dans la soirée** in the evening
**danse** dance
**danser** to dance

**date** date
**date de naissance** date of birth
**date d'expiration** expiry date
**date limite** deadline
**dater (de)** to date (from)
**de** of; from; **le vélo de David** David's bike; **de ... à ...** from ... to ...; **du pain** (some) bread; **des œufs** (some) eggs
**dé** dice
**début** beginning, start; **au début** at the beginning
**débutant** beginner
**décalage horaire** time difference; jetlag
**décapsuleur** bottle opener
**décembre** December
**décevant** disappointing
**décider** to decide
**déclaration** statement
**déclarer** to declare
**décoller** to take off
**déçu** disappointed
**dedans** inside
**défaut** flaw
**dégonflé** flat
**degré** degree
**dehors** outside
**déjà** already; yet
**déjeuner** *(n)* lunch; *(v)* to have lunch
**demain** tomorrow; **à demain !** see you tomorrow!; **demain soir** tomorrow evening
**demander** to ask
**démanger: ça me démange** it's itchy
**demi** half; **un demi-litre/-kilo** half a litre/kilo; **une demi-heure** half an hour; **une heure et demie** an hour and a half; **un demi** *(beer)* a half-pint
**demi-tour** U-turn
**demi-pension** half-board
**dent** tooth
**dentifrice** toothpaste
**dentiste** dentist

**déodorant** deodorant
**dépannage: service de dépannage** breakdown service
**départ** departure
**dépêcher: se dépêcher** to hurry (up)
**dépendre: ça dépend (de)** it depends (on)
**dépenser** to spend
**dépliant** leaflet
**déposer: déposer quelqu'un** to drop somebody off
**depuis** since; **depuis que** since; **depuis quand êtes-vous ici ?** how long have you been here?
**déranger** to disturb
**dernier** last; **au dernier moment** at the last minute; **l'année dernière** last year
**derrière** behind
**des** see de
**dès** from; **dès que** as soon as
**désagréable** unpleasant
**descendre** to go down; to get off
**désert** desert
**désinfecter** to disinfect
**désolé** sorry
**dessert** dessert
**dessous** underneath; **en dessous (de)** below
**dessus** above; **au-dessus (de)** above
**destinataire** addressee
**détendre: se détendre** to relax
**détester** to hate
**devant** in front of
**développer: faire développer une pellicule** to get a film developed
**devenir** to become
**devise** currency
**devoir** to have to; to owe; **je dois y aller** I have to go, I must go; **il doit être 5 heures** it must be 5 o'clock; **vous devriez ...** you should ...
**diabète** diabetes
**diapositive** slide

**diarrhée: avoir la diarrhée** to have diarrhoea

**diesel** diesel

**différent (de)** different (from)

**difficile (à)** difficult (to)

**dimanche** Sunday

**diminuer** to reduce

**dîner** *(n)* dinner; *(v)* to have dinner

**dire** to say; **vouloir dire** to mean; **comment dit-on … ?** how do you say …?; **ça te dit de … ?** do you feel like …?

**direct** direct

**directement** directly

**direction** direction; management; **le train en direction de Toulouse** the train to Toulouse

**discothèque** disco

**disque** record

**distributeur (automatique de billets)** cashpoint

**docteur** doctor

**document** document

**doigt** finger

**dommage: c'est dommage** it's a pity

**donc** so, therefore

**donner** to give

**dont** whose; **l'hôtel dont il me parlait** the hotel he told me about

**dormir** to sleep; **dormir à la belle étoile** to sleep out in the open

**dos** back

**douane** customs

**doublé** dubbed

**doucement** gently; softly; slowly

**douche** shower; **prendre une douche** to take a shower

**drap** sheet

**drogue** drug

**droit** *(n)* right; *(adj)* right; **le côté droit** the right-hand side; **avoir le droit de …** to have the right to …; **tout droit** straight on, straight ahead

**droite** right; **à droite (de)** to the right (of)

**drôle** funny

**du** see de

**dur** hard

**durer** to last

## E

**eau** water

**échanger** to exchange

**écharde** splinter

**écharpe** scarf

**écouter** to listen; **écouter quelqu'un/ quelque chose** to listen to someone/ something

**écrire** to write

**effort** effort; **faire un effort** to make an effort

**égal** equal; **ça m'est égal** I don't mind

**église** church

**électrique** electric

**elle** she; it

**elles** they; them

**embarquement** boarding

**embarquer** to board

**embouteillage** traffic jam

**embrayage** clutch

**émission** programme

**emmener** to take

**emplacement** spot, place

**emporter** to take; **à emporter** takeaway

**emprunter** to borrow

**en** in; **en France/2005/anglais** in France/2005/English; **je vais en France** I'm going to France; **en voiture** by car

**enceinte** pregnant

**enchanté!** pleased to meet you!

**encore** still; more; again; **pas encore** not yet; **encore plus** even more

**endormir: s'endormir** to fall asleep

**enfant** child

**enfin** finally

**enflé** swollen

**engueuler** to shout at; **s'engueuler** to have a row

**enlever** to remove

**ennuyer: s'enuyer** to be bored

**enregistrement** check-in

**enregistrer** to check in

**enrhumé: être enrhumé** to have a cold

**ensemble** together

**ensuite** then, next

**entendre** to hear

**entier** whole; **le gâteau en entier** the whole cake

**entracte** interval, intermission

**entre** between; **entre midi et deux** between midday and two

**entrée** entrance, way in; starter; admission

**entrer** to go in; to come in

**enveloppe** envelope

**envie: avoir envie de** to want to

**environ** about, around; **dans les environs** in the area

**envoyer** to send

**épaule** shoulder

**épicé** spicy, hot

**épicerie** grocer's

**éponge** sponge

**épuisé** exhausted; out of stock

**équipe** team

**erreur** mistake

**escalade** climbing

**escalier** stairs

**Espagne** Spain

**espagnol** Spanish

**espérer** to hope; **j'espère que …** I hope …

**essayer** to try; to try on; **essayer de faire quelque chose** to try to do something

**essence** petrol

**est** east; **à l'est** in the east; **à l'est de** (to the) east of

**estomac** stomach

**et** and

**étage** floor

**état** state

**États-Unis** United States

**été** summer

**éteindre** to put out; to switch off

**éternuer** to sneeze

**étonner** to surprise

**étranger** *(adj)* foreign; *(n)* foreigner; **à l'étranger** abroad

**être** to be; **je suis Écossais** I'm Scottish; **est-ce que tu es content ?** are you happy?; **c'est beau** it's beautiful

**études** studies; **faire des études de biologie** to study biology

**étudiant** student

**euro** euro

**eurochèque** Eurocheque

**Europe** Europe

**européen** European

**eux** them

**évanouir: s'évanouir** to faint

**évident** obvious

**excédent** excess; **j'avais un excédent de bagages de cinq kilos** my luggage was five kilos overweight

**exceptionnel** exceptional; **ça n'a rien d'exceptionnel** it's nothing special

**excursion** trip

**excuse** excuse

**excuser: s'excuser** to apologize; **excusez-moi** I'm sorry; excuse me

**exemple** example; **par exemple** for example

**expéditeur** sender

**expliquer** to explain

**exposition** exhibition

**exprès** on purpose

**exprimer** to express; **s'exprimer** to express oneself

**fac** university, uni
**face: en face (de)** opposite
**fâché** angry
**facile (à)** easy (to)
**façon** way; **de toute façon** anyway
**facteur** postman
**facture** bill
**faible** weak
**faim** hunger; **avoir faim** to be hungry
**faire** to do, to make; **ça ne fait rien** it doesn't matter
**fait** fact; **en fait** in fact; **au fait, ...** by the way ...; **fait main** handmade
**falaise** cliff
**falloir: il faut faire attention** you/we/etc must be careful; **il faut se dépêcher** we must hurry; **il me faut un stylo** I need a pen; **il faut que j'y aille** I must go; **il faut que vous le voyiez** you must see it
**famille** family
**fatigant** tiring
**fatigué** tired
**faute** mistake
**fauteuil roulant** wheelchair
**faux** wrong; false
**félicitations !** congratulations!
**femme** woman; wife
**fenêtre** window
**fer à repasser** iron
**férié: jour férié** public holiday; **lundi est férié** Monday is a public holiday
**fermé** closed, shut
**fermer** to close, to shut; **fermer à clé** to lock
**fermeture** closing; **heure de fermeture** closing time
**fermeture Éclair®** zip
**fesses** bottom
**festival** festival
**fête** party; **faire la fête** to celebrate; to have a good time

**fête foraine** funfair
**fête nationale** national holiday
**feu** fire; **tu as du feu ?** do you have a light?; **au feu !** fire!
**feu rouge** red light
**feux d'artifice** fireworks
**février** February
**fiancé** fiancé; **être fiancé** to be engaged
**fiancée** fiancée
**fier (de)** proud (of)
**fièvre** fever; **avoir de la fièvre** to have a temperature
**fille** girl; daughter
**film** film
**fils** son
**fin** (n) end; **à la fin de** at the end of
**fin** (adj) thin; fine
**finalement** finally
**finir** to finish
**fleuve** river
**flic** cop
**foie** liver
**foire** fair
**fois** time; **combien de fois ... ?** how many times ...?; **une/deux fois** once/twice
**folklorique** traditional
**foncé** dark; **bleu foncé** dark blue
**fond** bottom; **au fond de** at the bottom of; at the back of
**forêt** forest
**forfait** pass
**formulaire** form
**fort** strong; loud
**foulard** scarf
**fouler: se fouler la cheville** to sprain one's ankle
**four** oven
**fourchette** fork
**fourmi** ant
**fourrière** (car) pound
**fragile** fragile
**frais** cool; cold; chilly

**français** French
**France** France
**frein** brake
**frein à main** handbrake
**freiner** to brake
**frère** brother
**Frigidaire®** fridge
**frigo** fridge
**froid** cold; **il fait froid** it's cold; **avoir froid** to be cold; **prendre froid** to catch cold
**front** forehead
**fruit** piece of fruit; **fruits** fruit
**frontière** border
**fuite** leak
**fumer** to smoke
**fumeur** smoker; **fumeurs** smoking; **non-fumeurs** non-smoking
**fusible** fuse

# G

**gâcher** to waste
**gagner** to earn; to save
**galerie** gallery
**gant** glove
**gant de toilette** facecloth
**garage** garage
**garantie** guarantee
**garçon** boy; waiter
**garder** to keep
**gare** (train) station
**gare routière** coach station
**garer: se garer** to park
**gâter** to spoil
**gauche** left; **à gauche (de)** to the left (of)
**gaz** gas
**gazeux** fizzy
**gel** frost; gel
**gel douche** shower gel
**gendarme** policeman
**gendarmerie** police station
**généraliste** GP

**genou** knee
**genre: quel genre de … ?** what kind of …?
**gens** people; **les gens** people
**gentil** nice
**glace** ice; ice cream; mirror
**glaçon** ice cube; **avec ou sans glaçons ?** with or without ice?
**golf** golf; golf course
**gorge** throat
**gothique** Gothic
**gourde** flask
**goût** taste
**goûter** *(n)* (afternoon) snack
**goûter** to taste; to have an afternoon snack
**gouttes** drops
**grâce à** thanks to
**grammes** grams
**grand** big; tall
**Grande-Bretagne** (Great) Britain
**grandir** to grow; **j'ai grandi en France** I grew up in France
**grand-mère** grandmother
**grand-père** grandfather
**grands-parents** grandparents
**gras** fat
**grasse** fat
**gratte-ciel** skyscraper
**gratuit** free
**grave** serious; **ce n'est pas grave** it doesn't matter
**grec** Greek
**Grèce** Greece
**grippe** flu
**grippe intestinale** gastric flu
**gris** grey
**gros** big
**groupe** group; **groupe de musique** band
**guêpe** wasp
**guérir** to get better
**gueule de bois** hangover
**guide** guidebook; guide

**guide des spectacles** listings magazine
**gymnase** gym
**gynécologue** gynaecologist

**habiller: s'habiller** to get dressed
**habiter** to live
**habitude** habit; **d'habitude** usually;
   **j'ai l'habitude** I'm used to it
**hanche** hip
**handicapé** disabled
**haut** *(n)* top; **en haut** at the top;
   upstairs
**haut** *(adj)* high
**héberger** to put up
**hémorroïdes** piles
**herbe** grass
**hésiter** to hesitate
**heure** hour; **à quelle heure … ?** what
   time …?; **à cinq heures** at five o'clock;
   **à l'heure** on time; **heure locale** local
   time; **à tout à l'heure** see you later
**heureux** happy
**hier** yesterday; **hier soir** yesterday
   evening, last night
**histoire** history; story
**hiver** winter
**hollandais** Dutch
**Hollande** Holland, the Netherlands
**homéopathie** homoeopathy
**homme** man
**homosexuel** homosexual
**honnête** honest
**honte** shame; **avoir honte** to be
   ashamed
**hôpital** hospital
**horaires** timetable
**hors service** out of order
**hôtel** hotel
**hôtel de ville** town hall
**huile** oil
**humeur: être de bonne/mauvaise
   humeur** to be in a good/bad mood

**humide** damp
**humour** humour
**hypertension** high blood pressure
**hypotension** low blood pressure

**ici** here; **d'ici un quart d'heure** in a
   quarter of an hour
**il** he; it
**il y a: il y a un château** there is a
   castle; **il y a deux musées** there are
   two museums; **il y a deux ans** two
   years ago
**île** island
**ils** they
**immeuble** building; block of flats
**impatient** impatient; **être impatient
   de …** to be looking forward to …
**imperméable** *(adj)* waterproof
**imperméable** *(n)* raincoat
**important** important
**impossible** impossible
**imprimer** to print
**incendie** fire
**indépendant** independent
**indicatif** dialling code
**infection** infection
**infirmière** nurse
**informations** information; news
**inquiéter: s'inquiéter** to worry
**inscrire: s'inscrire** to sign up
**insecte** insect
**insecticide** insecticide
**insolation** sunstroke
**insomnie** insomnia
**instant: un instant, s'il vous plaît**
   one moment, please
**intention: avoir l'intention de** to
   intend to
**interdit** forbidden
**intérieur: à l'intérieur** inside
**intoxication alimentaire** food
   poisoning

**inutile** useless; **inutile de …** no need to …
**invité** (n) guest
**inviter** to invite
**Italie** Italy
**italien** Italian

## J

**jamais** never; **ne … jamais** never; **si jamais** if ever
**jambe** leg
**janvier** January
**Japon** Japan
**japonais** Japanese
**jardin** garden
**jaune** yellow
**je** I
**jean** jeans
**jetable** disposable
**jeter** to throw; to throw out
**jeudi** Thursday
**jeune** (adj) young
**jeune** (n) young person
**jogging** jogging; tracksuit
**joli** pretty
**jouer** to play; **jouer à** to play; **ça joue à …** it's on at …
**jouet** toy
**jour** day; **de nos jours** nowadays
**journal** newspaper
**journée** day
**juillet** July
**juin** June
**jumelles** binoculars
**jupe** skirt
**jusqu'à** until
**juste** fair; **juste avant/un peu** just before/a little

## K

**kilomètre** kilometre
**kiosque à journaux** newsstand

**K-way®** waterproof jacket

## L

**la** the; her; it
**là** there
**là-bas** over there
**lac** lake
**là-haut** up there; upstairs
**laine** wool
**laisser** to let; to leave; **laissez-moi tranquille** leave me alone; **laisser tomber** to drop
**lait après-soleil** after-sun
**lait hydratant** moisturizer
**lame de rasoir** razor blade
**lampe** lamp
**lampe de poche** torch
**langue** tongue; language
**large** wide
**lavabo** washbasin
**lave-vaisselle** dishwasher
**laver** to wash; **se laver** to have a wash; **se laver les dents** to clean one's teeth; **se laver les cheveux** to wash one's hair
**laverie** launderette
**le** the; him; it
**léger** light
**lentement** slowly
**lentilles** lentils; **lentilles (de contact)** contact lenses
**les** the; them
**lessive** washing powder
**lettre** letter
**leur** (adj) their; (pron) them; **leurs** their; **le/la leur, les leurs** theirs
**lever: se lever** to get up
**levée** collection
**lever du soleil** sunrise
**lèvre** lip
**librairie** bookshop
**libre** available; free
**lieu** place; **au lieu de** instead of

**ligne** line; **ligne de métro** underground line; **ligne de bus** bus route

**linge sale** (dirty) washing

**liquide** cash; **payer en liquide** to pay cash

**liquide vaisselle** washing-up liquid

**lire** to read

**lit** bed

**litre** litre

**livre** book

**livre (sterling)** pound

**location** rental, hire

**logement** accommodation

**loin** far; **loin de** far from

**longtemps** a long time

**lorsque** when

**louer** to rent, to hire

**lourd** heavy; close

**loyer** rent

**lui** him; her; it

**lumière** light

**lundi** Monday

**lune** moon

**lune de miel** honeymoon

**lunettes** glasses

**lunettes de soleil** sunglasses

**luxe** luxury; **... de luxe** luxury ...

# M

**ma** my

**machine à laver** washing machine

**Madame** Mrs; Madam

**Mademoiselle** Miss

**magasin** shop; **grand magasin** department store

**mai** May

**maigre** thin

**maillot de bain** swimsuit; swimming trunks

**main** hand

**maintenant** now

**mairie** town hall

**mais** but

**maison** house; **à la maison** at home

**mal** (adj) bad; (adv) badly; **ça fait mal** it hurts; **avoir mal au cœur** to feel sick; **avoir mal à la tête/à la gorge/ au ventre** to have a headache/a sore throat/a sore stomach; **avoir le mal de mer** to be seasick; **avoir du mal à faire quelque chose** to have trouble doing something; **c'est pas mal** it's not bad; **pas mal de** quite a lot of

**malade** ill

**maladie** illness

**malentendu** misunderstanding

**maman** mum, mummy

**manche** sleeve

**Manche: la Manche** the (English) Channel

**mandat international** international money order

**manger** to eat

**manière** way; **de toute manière** in any case

**manquer** to miss; **il manque deux ...** there are two ... missing; **il me manque deux ...** I'm two ... short; **tu me manques** I miss you

**manteau** coat

**maquillage** make-up

**maquiller: se maquiller** to put on one's make-up

**marchand** shopkeeper

**marchand de journaux** newsagent

**marchandises** goods

**marche** step; **faire de la marche** to go walking; **marche avant/arrière** forward/reverse gear

**marché** market

**marcher** to walk; to work

**mardi** Tuesday

**marée basse/haute** low/high tide

**mari** husband

**mariage** wedding; marriage

**marié** married

**marre: en avoir marre (de)** to be fed up (with)
**marron** brown; chestnut
**mars** March
**match** match
**matelas** mattress
**matelas pneumatique** airbed
**matériel** equipment
**matin** morning
**mauvais** bad; **il fait mauvais** the weather's bad
**me** me
**mec** guy
**méchant** bad
**médecin** doctor
**médicament** medicine
**meilleur** better; **le meilleur** the best; the better; **meilleur que ...** better than ...
**mélanger** to mix
**membre** member
**même** *(adj)* same; *(adv)* even; **même si** even if; **moi-même** myself; **lui-même** himself
**ménage** housework; **faire le ménage** to do the housework
**mentir** to lie
**menton** chin
**menu** set menu
**mer** sea; **la mer Méditerranée/du Nord** the Mediterranean/North Sea
**merci** thank you, thanks; **merci beaucoup** thank you very much; **non merci** no, thank you
**mercredi** Wednesday
**mère** mother
**mes** my
**message** message
**messe** mass
**métier** occupation
**mètre** metre
**métro** underground
**mettre** to put
**micro-ondes** microwave

**midi** midday, noon
**mien: le mien/la mienne** mine; **les miens/miennes** mine
**mieux** better; **mieux que ...** better than ...
**mignon** cute, pretty
**milieu** middle; **au milieu (de)** in the middle (of)
**ministre** minister
**minuit** midnight
**minute** minute
**Mobylette®** moped
**moderne** modern
**moi** me
**moins** less; **au moins** at least; **moins que** less than; **dix heures moins le quart** a quarter to ten
**mois** month
**moitié** half
**moment** moment; **un moment !** just a moment!; **en ce moment** at the moment; **pour le moment** for the moment; **à ce moment-là** then
**mon** my
**monastère** monastery
**monde** world; **tout le monde** everybody; **il y a du monde** there are lots of people
**monnaie** money; currency; change
**Monsieur** Mr; Sir
**montagne** mountain
**montre** watch
**montrer** to show
**monument** monument
**morceau** piece; **un morceau de** a piece of
**morsure** bite
**mort** *(adj)* dead; *(n)* dead
**mosquée** mosque
**mot** word; note
**moteur** engine
**moto** motorcycle, motorbike
**mouche** fly
**mouchoir** handkerchief

**mouillé** wet
**moulin** mill
**mourir** to die
**mousse à raser** shaving foam
**moustique** mosquito
**moyen** *(n)* way; *(adj)* average
**mur** wall
**mûr** ripe
**muscle** muscle
**musée** museum
**musique** music

# N

**nager** to swim; **est-ce que tu sais nager?** can you swim?
**naître: je suis né le/en …** I was born on the/in …
**natation** swimming
**nature** nature
**nausée: avoir la nausée** to feel sick
**navette** shuttle
**ne** see **pas**, **plus**, **jamais**, **rien**
**né** see **naître**
**nécessaire** necessary
**négatif** negative
**neige** snow
**neiger** to snow
**nerveux** nervous
**nettoyer** to clean
**neuf** nine; new
**neuve** new
**neveu** nephew
**nez** nose
**ni … ni …** neither … nor …
**nièce** niece
**nocturne** *(n)* late-night opening
**Noël** Christmas; **joyeux Noël !** Merry Christmas!
**noir** black; **noir et blanc** black and white
**nom** name; surname
**nombre** number
**nom de famille** surname

**nom de jeune fille** maiden name
**non** no; **je ne fume pas — moi non plus** I don't smoke — neither do I
**nord** north; **au nord** in the north; **au nord de** (to the) north of
**normal** normal
**nos** our
**note** bill
**noter** to write down
**notre** our
**nôtre: le/la nôtre** ours; **les nôtres** ours
**nourriture** food
**nous** we; us
**nouveau** new; **de/à nouveau** again; **nouvel an** New Year
**nouvelle** *(adj)* new
**nouvelle:** *(n)* **bonne/mauvaise nouvelle** good/bad news; **les nouvelles** the news
**novembre** November
**noyer: se noyer** to drown
**nu** naked
**nuage** cloud
**nuit** night; **bonne nuit** goodnight
**nul** useless; **nulle part** nowhere
**numéro** number
**numéro de téléphone** phone number
**numéro d'immatriculation** registration number

# O

**objectif** lens
**occasion** opportunity; **d'occasion** second-hand
**occupé** busy; engaged
**occuper: s'occuper de** to look after
**océan** ocean; **l'océan Atlantique** the Atlantic Ocean
**octobre** October
**odeur** smell
**œil** eye
**œuf** egg

**œuvre d'art** work of art
**office de tourisme** tourist office
**offrir** to offer; to give
**oiseau** bird
**ombre** shade; **à l'ombre** in the shade
**on** one; we; **on dit que …** they say that …
**oncle** uncle
**ongle** nail
**opérer** to operate; **se faire opérer** to have an operation
**opticien** optician
**orage** storm
**orange** orange
**orchestre** orchestra
**ordinateur** computer
**ordinateur portable** laptop
**ordures** rubbish
**oreille** ear
**oreiller** pillow
**organiser** to organize
**origine** origin; **être d'origine …** to be of … origin
**ou** or
**où** where; **où est/sont … ?** where is/are?; **où vas-tu ?** where are you going?; **d'où viens-tu ?** where are you from?
**oublier** to forget
**ouest** west; **à l'ouest** in the west; **à l'ouest de** (to the) west of
**oui** yes
**ouvert** open
**ouvre-boîtes** can opener
**ouvre-bouteilles** bottle opener
**ouvrir** to open

---

### P

**page** page
**palais** palace
**pâle** pale
**panier** basket
**panne** breakdown; **tomber en panne**

to break down; **être en panne d'essence** to have run out of petrol
**panneau** sign; road sign
**pansement** dressing, Elastoplast®
**pantalon** trousers
**papa** dad, daddy
**papier** paper
**papier à cigarette** cigarette paper
**papier alu** tinfoil
**papier cadeau** gift wrap
**papiers d'identité** identity papers
**papier toilette** toilet paper
**Pâques** Easter; **joyeuses Pâques !** Happy Easter!
**paquet** packet; parcel
**paraître: il paraît que …** it seems that …
**par** by; **une fois par jour/heure** once a day/an hour
**parapluie** umbrella
**parasol** beach umbrella
**parc** park
**parc d'attractions** theme park
**parce que** because
**pardon** sorry; excuse me
**pare-brise** windscreen
**pare-chocs** bumper
**pareil** same
**parents** parents
**parfum** perfume; flavour
**parking** car park
**parler** to speak
**parmi** among
**partager** to share
**partie** part; **faire partie de** to be a part of
**partir** to leave; **à partir de …** from …
**partout** everywhere
**pas: ne … pas** not; **pas du tout** not at all
**passage: être de passage** to be passing through
**passager** passenger
**passé** *(n)* past

**passeport** passport

**passer** to spend; **je suis passé vers 6 heures** I came by around 6 o'clock; **passer prendre quelqu'un** to go and pick somebody up; **passer un coup de téléphone** to make a phone call; **se passer de …** to go without …

**patient** patient

**pâtisserie** pastry; cake shop

**patron** boss

**pauvre** poor

**payant: l'entrée est payante** there's a charge for admission

**payer** to pay

**pays** country

**paysage** landscape; scenery

**Pays-Bas** Netherlands

**PCV** reverse charge call

**péage** toll

**peau** skin

**pêcher** to fish

**peigne** comb

**peine: à peine** hardly; **ça vaut la peine** it's worth it

**peinture** painting

**peler** to peel

**pellicule** film

**pendant** during; **pendant une heure** for an hour; **pendant que** while

**pension complète** full board

**penser** to think; **penser à** to think about

**perdre** to lose; **se perdre** to get lost; **être perdu** to be lost; **perdre du temps** to waste time

**père** father

**périmé** out of date

**permettre** to allow

**permis de conduire** driving licence

**personne** (n) person; (pron) nobody

**petit** small, little; **petit à petit** little by little

**petit déjeuner** (n) breakfast

**peu** not much; not very; few; **peu de** few, not many; little, not much; **un peu** a little; **un peu de vin** a little wine; **à peu près** almost; around

**peuple** people

**peur** fear; **avoir peur (de)** to be scared (of)

**peut-être** maybe, perhaps

**phare** lighthouse; headlight

**pharmacie** chemist's

**pharmacie de garde** duty chemist's

**photo** photo; **prendre quelqu'un en photo** to take somebody's photo; **prendre une/des photo(s)** to take a photo/photos

**pièce** coin; room

**pièce de rechange** spare part

**pièce de théâtre** play

**pied** foot; **aller à pied** to walk, to go on foot

**pierre** stone

**piéton** pedestrian; **rue piétonne** pedestrian street

**pile** battery; **trois heures pile** three o'clock on the dot

**pilule** pill; **prendre la pilule** to be on the pill

**pilule du lendemain** morning-after pill

**pipe** pipe

**pipi** pee; **faire pipi** to have a pee

**pique-nique** picnic

**pique-niquer** to have a picnic

**piquer** to sting; **se faire piquer (par)** to get stung (by)

**piqûre** injection; sting

**pire** worse; **c'est pire (que)** it's worse (than)

**piscine** swimming pool

**piste cyclable** cycle path

**place** seat; square; **il n'y a plus de place** there's no more room; there are no seats/tickets left; **sur place** on the spot

**place de parking** parking space

**plage** beach

**plaie** wound
**plaindre: se plaindre** to complain
**plaire** to please; **s'il te/vous plaît** please; **ça me plaît** I like it
**plan** map
**planche à voile** windsurfing
**planche de surf** surfboard
**plante** plant
**plaque électrique** hotplate
**plat** *(adj)* flat
**plat** *(n)* dish
**plat du jour** today's special
**plat principal** main course
**plâtre: avoir la jambe dans le plâtre** to have one's leg in plaster
**plein** full; **plein de** full of; **faire le plein (d'essence)** to fill up (with petrol)
**pleuvoir: il pleut** it's raining
**plombage** filling
**plombier** plumber
**plongée (sous-marine)** (scuba) diving; **faire de la plongée** to go diving
**pluie** rain
**plupart: la plupart** most; **la plupart des gens** most people
**plus** more; **il n'y a plus de …** there's/there are no more …; **il ne me reste plus que deux jours** I have only two days left; **ce que j'ai le plus aimé** what I liked most
**plusieurs** several
**plutôt** rather
**pneu** tyre
**poêle** frying pan
**poignet** wrist
**poil** hair
**point** point; **être sur le point de …** to be about to …; **à point** medium
**pointure** size
**poisson** fish
**poissonnerie** fishmonger's
**poitrine** chest
**police** police
**policier** policeman

**pommade** ointment
**pompe à vélo** bicycle pump
**pompiers** fire brigade
**pont** bridge
**port** port; harbour; **port de plaisance** marina
**portable** mobile (phone)
**porte** door; gate
**portefeuille** wallet
**porte-monnaie** purse
**porter** to carry; to wear
**portrait** portrait
**portugais** Portuguese
**Portugal** Portugal
**poser** to put; **poser une question** to ask a question
**possible** possible; **le plus tôt possible** as soon as possible
**poste** mail, post; post office
**pot** pot; jar
**potable: eau potable** drinking water; **eau non potable** non-drinking water
**pot d'échappement** exhaust (pipe)
**poubelle** (dust)bin; **mettre à la poubelle** to throw out
**poudre** powder
**poumon** lung
**pour** for; **pour que** so that; **pour cent** percent; **être pour quelque chose** to be in favour of something
**pourboire** tip
**pourquoi** why
**pousser** to push
**poussette** pushchair
**pouvoir** to be able to; **je ne peux pas** I can't; **on peut y aller demain** we can go tomorrow
**pratique** practical
**précédent** previous
**préféré** favourite
**préférer** to prefer
**premier** first
**prendre** to take; **ça prend deux heures** it takes two hours

**prénom** first name
**préparer** to prepare
**près** near; **(tout) près de** (right) beside
**présenter** to introduce; **je te présente …** this is …
**préservatif** condom
**presque** almost
**pressé: être pressé** to be in a hurry
**pressing** dry cleaner's
**pression** (draught) beer; pressure
**prêt** ready; **être prêt à** to be ready to
**prêter** to lend
**prévenir** to warn
**prévisions météo** weather forecast
**prévoir** to plan; to forecast
**prier: je t'en/vous en prie** you're welcome
**principal** main
**printemps** spring
**prise** socket; plug
**privé** private
**prix** price; prize
**probablement** probably
**problème** problem
**prochain** next; **à la prochaine !** see you (soon)!
**proche** near; **le plus proche** the nearest
**produit** product
**profession** profession
**profiter de** to make the most of
**profond** deep
**promener: se promener** to walk; **aller se promener** to go for a walk
**promettre** to promise
**proposer** to suggest
**propre** clean; own
**propriétaire** owner
**protéger** to protect; **se protéger** to protect oneself
**prudent** careful
**public** *(adj)* public; *(n)* public
**puisque** since

**pull** sweater, jumper
**pyjama** (pair of) pyjamas

 **Q**

**quai** platform; quay
**qualité** quality; **de bonne qualité** of good quality
**quand** when; **quand même** all the same
**quart** quarter; **un quart d'heure** a quarter of an hour
**quartier** area
**que** that; **ne … que** only; **que veux-tu ?** what do you want?; **qu'est-ce que … ?** what …?; **plus petit que** smaller than; **je pense que …** I think (that) …
**quel** what, which
**quelque chose** something
**quelque part** somewhere
**quelquefois** sometimes
**quelques** some
**quelques-uns** some
**quelqu'un** someone, somebody
**question** question; **poser une question** to ask a question
**queue** tail; queue; **faire la queue** to queue (up)
**qui** who
**quitter** to leave; **ne quittez pas** hold on
**quoi** what; **il n'y a pas de quoi** you're welcome
**quoique** although

**R**

**rabais : faire un rabais à quelqu'un** to give somebody a discount
**raccourci** short cut
**raconter** to tell
**radiateur** radiator
**radio** radio; X-ray

**rage de dents** severe toothache
**raisonnable** reasonable
**râler** to moan
**randonnée** hiking, hill-walking; **faire de la randonnée** to go hiking/hill-walking
**ranger** to tidy
**rapide** quick
**rappeler** to call back; **se rappeler** to remember; **ça me rappelle …** that reminds me of …
**raquette** racket
**rare** rare
**rarement** rarely
**raser: se raser** to shave
**rasoir** razor
**rasoir électrique** electric shaver
**rater** to miss
**ravi** delighted; **ravi de faire votre connaissance** pleased to meet you
**rayon** department
**réception** reception; signal; **à la réception** at reception
**recette** recipe
**recevoir** to receive, to get
**rechange: … de rechange** spare …
**recharger** to charge
**recommandé: en recommandé** registered
**recommander** to recommend
**reconnaissant** grateful
**reconnaître** to recognize
**reçu** receipt
**réduction** reduction
**réfléchir** to think
**réfrigérateur** fridge
**refuge de montagne** mountain hut
**refuser** to refuse
**regarder** to look at, to watch
**régime** diet; **être au régime** to be on a diet
**région** area; **dans la région** in the area
**règles** periods; **avoir ses règles** to be having one's period

**rein** kidney
**rejoindre** to meet
**remarquer** to notice
**rembourser** to refund; **se faire rembourser** to get a refund
**remercier** to thank
**remontée mécanique** ski lift
**remplir** to fill; to fill in/out
**rencontrer** to meet; **se rencontrer** to meet (each other)
**rendez-vous** appointment; date; **prendre un rendez-vous** to make an appointment; **se donner rendez-vous** to arrange to meet; **avoir rendez-vous (avec)** to meet; to have an appointment (with)
**rendre** to give back
**renseignement** information; **les renseignements** directory enquiries
**rentrer** to go home
**renverser** to knock over; **se faire renverser** to get knocked down
**réparer** to repair; **faire réparer** to get repaired
**repas** meal
**repasser** to iron
**repère** landmark; **point de repère** landmark
**répéter** to repeat
**répondeur** answering machine
**répondre** to answer
**réponse** answer
**reposer: se reposer** to rest
**réservé** reserved
**réserver** to book
**ressembler à** to look like
**reste** rest; **le reste** the rest
**rester** to stay; **est-ce qu'il reste des places ?** are there any tickets left?
**retard** delay; **en retard** late
**retardé** delayed
**retirer** to withdraw
**retour** return; **être de retour** to be back

**retrait des bagages** baggage reclaim
**retrouver: se retrouver** to meet
**réunion** meeting
**réveil** alarm clock
**réveiller** to wake up; **se réveiller** to wake up
**revenir** to come back
**rêver** to dream
**revoir: au revoir** goodbye
**revoir: se revoir** to see each other again
**revue** magazine
**rez-de-chaussée** ground floor
**rhumatismes** rheumatism
**rhume** cold
**rhume des foins** hay fever
**riche** rich
**rien: ne rien** nothing
**rigoler** to laugh; to joke
**rire** to laugh
**risque** risk
**risquer: il risque de pleuvoir** it might rain
**rivière** river
**robe** dress
**rocher** rock
**rollers** rollerblades
**roman** *(n)* novel
**roman** *(adj)* Romanesque
**rond-point** roundabout
**robinet** tap
**robinet d'arrêt** stopcock
**rose** pink; rose
**roue** wheel; **roue avant** front wheel
**roue de secours** spare wheel
**rouge** red
**route** road
**rouvrir** to reopen
**Royaume-Uni** United Kingdom
**rue** street
**ruines** ruins; **en ruines** in ruins

**sa** his; her
**sable** sand
**sac** bag
**sac à dos** backpack, rucksack
**sac à main** handbag
**sac de couchage** sleeping bag
**sac plastique** plastic bag
**sac poubelle** bin bag
**saignant** rare
**saigner** to bleed
**saison** season
**sale** dirty
**salé** salted; salty; savoury
**salir** to (get) dirty; **se salir** to get dirty
**salle** room
**salle de cinéma** auditorium
**salle de concert** concert hall
**salle de bains** bathroom
**salon** living room
**salut!** hi!; bye!
**samedi** Saturday
**sandales** sandals
**sang** blood
**sans** without
**santé** health; **être en bonne santé** to be in good health; **santé !** cheers!
**sauf** except
**sauvage** wild
**sauvegarder** to save
**savoir** to know; **sais-tu nager ?** can you swim?
**savon** soap
**Scotch®** Sellotape®
**sec** dry
**sèche** dry
**sèche-cheveux** hairdrier
**sécher** to dry; **faire sécher** to dry
**seconde** second
**secours** help; **au secours !** help!; **appeler au secours** to call for help
**secrétaire** secretary

**sécurité** security, safety; **en sécurité** secure, safe

**sein** breast

**séjour** stay

**sel** salt

**semaine** week; **en semaine** during the week; **toute la semaine** all week

**sens** direction; sense, meaning

**sensible** sensitive

**sentier** path

**sentiment** feeling

**sentir** to feel; to smell; **sentir bon/ mauvais** to smell good/bad; **se sentir** to feel; **se sentir bien/mal** to feel good/bad

**séparer** to separate; **se séparer** to split up

**septembre** September

**sérieux** serious

**serré** tight

**serrure** lock

**serveur** barman; waiter

**serveuse** barmaid; waitress

**service** tip; favour; **rendre service à quelqu'un** to do somebody a favour

**serviette** towel; napkin

**serviette de bain** bath towel

**serviette en papier** paper napkin

**serviette hygiénique** sanitary towel

**servir à** to be used for; **se servir de** to use

**ses** his; her

**seul** only; alone; **un seul** just one; **voyager seul** to travel alone

**seulement** only

**sexe** sex

**shampooing** shampoo

**shopping** shopping; **aller faire du shopping** to go shopping

**short** (pair of) shorts

**si** so; if; yes

**siècle** century; **au XIX° siècle** in the 19th century

**sien: le sien/la sienne** his; hers; **les siens/siennes** his; hers

**sieste** nap; **faire la sieste** to have a nap

**signer** to sign

**signifier** to mean

**silent** silencieux

**simple** simple

**sinon** otherwise

**sirop** syrup

**site Internet** website

**ski** ski; skiing; **faire du ski** to go skiing

**ski nautique** waterskiing

**slip** pants

**slip de bain** swimming trunks

**SMS** text message

**société** company; society

**sœur** sister

**soif** thirst; **avoir soif** to be thirsty

**soir** evening; **ce soir** this evening, tonight; **le soir** in the evening(s)

**soirée** evening; party; **dans la soirée** in the evening

**sol** ground; floor

**soldes** sales; **en solde** in the sale

**soleil** sun; **au soleil** in the sun

**sommeil** sleep; **avoir sommeil** to be sleepy

**sommet** top, summit

**somnifère** sleeping pill

**son** his; her

**sortie** exit, way out

**sortie de secours** emergency exit

**sortir** to go out; to come out; **sortir avec quelqu'un** to go out with somebody; **sortir les poubelles** to take the rubbish out

**souci** worry; **se faire du souci (pour)** to worry (about)

**souffrir** to suffer

**souhait** wish; **à tes/vos souhaits !** bless you!

**soûl** drunk

**sourd** deaf

**sourire** (v) to smile; (n) smile

**souris** mouse
**sous** under
**sous-titré** subtitled
**sous-vêtements** underwear
**soutien-gorge** bra
**souvenir** memory; souvenir; **en souvenir de** in memory of; **se souvenir (de)** to remember
**souvent** often; **pas souvent** seldom
**sparadrap** sticking plaster
**spécial** special
**spécialité** speciality
**spectacle** show
**sport** sport
**sportif** sporty
**stade** stadium
**standardiste** (switchboard) operator
**station balnéaire** seaside resort
**station de métro** tube station
**station de radio** radio station
**station de ski** ski resort
**station-service** petrol station
**stérilet** coil
**stop** hitchhiking; **faire du stop** to hitchhike
**stylo** pen
**succès** success
**sucre** sugar
**sucré** sweet
**sucreries** sweet things
**sud** south; **au sud** in the south; **au sud de** (to the) south of
**suffire** to be enough; **ça suffit** that's enough
**suivant** next
**suivre** to follow; **faire suivre** to forward
**super** *(adj)* great
**super** *(n)* four-star petrol
**supermarché** supermarket
**supplémentaire** extra
**supporter** to put up with; **je ne supporte pas …** I can't stand …
**sur** on; over

**sûr** sure; **être sûr** to be sure; **bien sûr** of course
**surf** surfing; **faire du surf** to go surfing
**surfer** to surf
**surprise** surprise
**surveiller** to look after
**sympa** nice

# T

**ta** your
**tabac** tobacco; tobacconist's
**table** table
**tableau** painting
**tache** stain
**taie d'oreiller** pillowcase
**taille** size; waist
**tampon** tampon
**tant: tant mieux** all the better; **tant pis** too bad
**tante** aunt
**tapis** rug
**tapis de sol** groundsheet
**tard** late; **à plus tard !** see you later!
**tarif** price, fare; **plein tarif** full price/fare; **tarif réduit** concession
**tasse** cup, mug
**taux de change** exchange rate
**taxe** tax; **taxe d'aéroport** airport tax; **hors taxes** tax-free
**taxi** taxi
**te** you
**tee-shirt** T-shirt
**télé** TV
**téléphone** telephone
**téléphone portable** mobile (phone)
**téléphoner (à)** to (tele)phone
**télésiège** chairlift
**télévision** television
**température** temperature; **prendre sa température** to take one's temperature
**tempête** storm
**temple** temple; (Protestant) church

**temporaire** temporary
**temps** weather; time; **de temps en temps** from time to time; **tout le temps** all the time; **ces derniers temps** lately; **avoir le temps de** to have (the) time to
**tenir** to hold
**tennis** trainers
**tension** tension; stress; blood pressure
**tente** tent
**terrain de camping** campsite
**terrain de golf** golf course
**terrain de sport** sports ground
**terrasse** terrace; pavement area; **en terrasse** outside
**terre** earth; **par terre** on the ground/floor
**tes** your
**tête** head
**théâtre** theatre
**thermomètre** thermometer
**ticket** ticket
**ticket de caisse** receipt
**tiède** lukewarm
**tien: le tien/la tienne** yours; **les tiens/tiennes** yours
**timbre** stamp
**timide** shy
**tire-bouchon** corkscrew
**tire-fesses** T-bar
**tirer** to pull
**tissu** material
**toi** you
**toilettes** toilet; **toilettes pour hommes** gents'; **toilettes pour femmes** ladies'; **affaires de toilette** toiletries
**tomber** to fall; **tomber malade** to fall ill
**ton** your
**tongs** flip-flops
**torchon** dish towel
**tôt** early
**toucher** to touch

**toujours** always; still
**touriste** tourist
**touristique** tourist
**tournée** round
**tourner** to turn
**tous** all; **tous/toutes les deux** both; **tous les jours** every day
**tousser** to cough
**tout** all; **tout le temps** all the time; **tout le monde** everybody; **toute la journée** all day; **tout de suite** right away; **tout droit** straight ahead
**toutes** see **tous**
**toux** cough; **avoir de la toux** to have a cough
**traditionnel** traditional
**traduire** to translate
**train** train
**tramway** tram
**tranche** slice
**tranquille** quiet
**transat** deckchair
**transpirer** to sweat
**travail** work, job
**travailler** to work; **travailler dans** to work in
**travaux** works; roadworks
**travers: à travers** across
**traverser** to cross
**très** very
**tromper: se tromper** to make a mistake
**trop** too; too much; too many; **trop de** too much; too many
**trou** hole
**trousse de toilette** toilet bag
**trouver** to find; **trouver quelque chose difficile** to find something difficult
**truc** thing
**tu** you
**tuer** to kill
**tupperware** tupperware
**TVA** VAT

**type** type; guy

**un, une** a, an; one
**Union européenne** European Union
**université** university
**urgence** emergency; **en cas d'urgence** in an emergency; **appeler les urgences** to call the emergency services
**urgent** urgent
**utile** useful
**utiliser** to use

## V

**vacances** holiday(s); **en vacances** on holiday
**vacciner: être vacciné contre** to be vaccinated against
**vague** wave
**vaisselle** dishes; **faire la vaisselle** to do the dishes
**valable (pour)** valid (for)
**validité: en cours de validité** valid
**valise** suitcase; **faire ses valises** to pack one's bags
**vallée** valley
**valoir** to be worth; **ça vaut ...** it's worth ...; **il vaut mieux ...** it's better to ...
**végétarien** vegetarian
**vélo** bike
**vendeur** shop assistant
**vendre** to sell; **à vendre** for sale
**vendredi** Friday
**venir** to come; **je viens de Paris** I come from Paris; **je viens d'arriver** I've just arrived
**vent** wind
**ventilateur** fan
**ventre** stomach
**vérifier** to check

**verre** glass; **verre d'eau/de vin** glass of water/of wine; **prendre un verre** to have a drink
**verrou** lock
**vers** towards
**version: en version originale** in the original language
**vert** green
**veste** jacket
**vestiaire** cloakroom
**vêtement** piece of clothing; **vêtements** clothes
**vide** empty
**vie** life
**vieille** old
**vieux** old; **les vieux** old people
**village** village
**ville** town; city; **vieille ville** old town
**vin** wine; **vin blanc/rouge** white/red wine
**viol** rape
**violer** to rape
**violence** violence
**violent** violent
**violet** purple
**virement** (bank) transfer
**visa** visa
**visite** visit; **rendre visite à ...** to visit ...
**visite guidée** guided tour
**visiter** to visit
**vite** fast, quickly
**vitesse** speed; **à toute vitesse** at full speed
**vitraux** stained-glass windows
**vitre** window
**vitrine: en vitrine** in the window
**vivant** living; alive
**vivre** to live
**vœux: meilleurs vœux** best wishes
**voici** here is/are
**voilà** there is/are
**voile** sail; sailing; **faire de la voile** to go sailing; **bateau à voile** sailing boat

**voir** to see

**voisin** neighbour

**voiture** car; coach; **en voiture** by car

**voix** voice; **à voix haute** aloud; **à voix basse** in a low voice

**vol** theft; flight

**voler** to steal; to fly

**voleur** thief

**vomir** to vomit; **avoir envie de vomir** to feel sick

**vos** your

**votre** your

**vôtre: le/la vôtre** yours; **les vôtres** yours

**vouloir** to want; **vouloir dire** to mean; **je voudrais …** I'd like …

**vous** you

**voyage** journey, trip; **bon voyage !** have a good trip!

**voyage d'affaires** business trip

**voyage de noces** honeymoon

**voyage organisé** package holiday

**voyager** to travel

**voyelle** vowel

**vrai** true; real

**vraiment** really

**VTT** mountain bike

**vue** view; **vue panoramique** panoramic view; **vue sur mer** sea view

## WYZ

**week-end** weekend

**y** there; **il y a** there is/are

**yeux** eyes

**zéro** zero

**zoo** zoo

**zoom** zoom (lens)

# GRAMMAR

French has two ways of saying *you* but these cover four situations: **polite** and **informal**, each in the singular and the plural. Use the informal form when speaking to friends or children, and the polite form to strangers, older people, or people in authority. In the singular, ie when you are speaking to just one person, the informal form is **tu** and the polite form is **vous**. The plural for both of these is **vous**, used when you are speaking to more than one person. So, when asking *how are you*:

|          | Singular                | Plural                  |
|----------|-------------------------|-------------------------|
|          | **comment vas-tu ?**    | **comment allez-vous ?**|
| Informal | **comment vas-tu ?**    | **comment allez-vous ?**|
| Polite   | **comment allez-vous ?**| **comment allez-vous ?**|

There are two ways of converting a statement into a **question** in French:
- by putting **est-ce que** (**est-ce qu'** when the first word of the statement starts with a vowel) in front of the statement:

> **leur mère habite en France** their mother lives in France
> **est-ce que leur mère habite en France ?** does their mother live in France?
> **est-ce qu'elle habite en France ?** does she live in France?

- by inverting the verb and the subject and putting a hyphen between the two:

> **elle est à la maison** she's at home
> **est-elle à la maison ?** is she at home?
> **leur mère est à la maison** their mother's at home
> **leur mère est-elle à la maison ?** is their mother at home?

The first method is often easier to use than the second. In many situations, a statement can be turned into a question simply by using a rising intonation at the end of the statement:

> **leur mère habite en France ?** does their mother live in France?

To make a sentence **negative**, insert **ne** (**n'** before a vowel) before the verb and **pas** after it:

> **Cécile vient demain** Cécile's coming tomorrow
> **Cécile ne vient pas demain** Cécile's not coming tomorrow

Negatives with *never* are formed with **ne** and **jamais**:

> **il n'appelle jamais** he never phones

Negatives with *nothing/not anything* are formed with **ne** and **rien**:

> **je ne vois rien** I can see nothing, I can't see anything
> **elle n'a rien dit** she said nothing, she didn't say anything

French **nouns** are either **masculine** or **feminine**.

The **definite article** (*the* in English) and **indefinite article** (*a/an* in English) vary according to whether the noun is masculine or feminine, singular or plural:

|  | masc. sing. | masc. pl. | fem. sing. | fem. pl. |
|---|---|---|---|---|
| definite | le | les | la | les |
| indefinite | un | des | une | des |

> **le garçon** the boy, **les garçons** the boys, **un garçon** a boy, **des garçons** some boys
> **la fille** the girl, **les filles** the girls, **une fille** a girl, **des filles** some girls

Note that **le** and **la** become **l'** before a word beginning with a vowel:

> **l'enfant** the child

The French for *some* is **du** in the masculine singular, **de la** in the feminine singular and **des** in the plural:

> **j'ai du vin** I've got some wine
> **j'ai de la glace** I've got some ice cream
> **j'ai des verres** I've got some glasses

In French a noun is virtually never used on its own without **le/la/les/du/de la/des** before it, so:

> **j'aime le vin blanc** I like white wine
> **j'aime les fraises** I like strawberries

In some case, the ending of a noun is a good indication of its **gender**.

- Words of more than one syllable with the following endings are generally masculine: -age, -ail, -eau, -et, -isme, -ège, -ème, -ment.
  **le chauffage** (heating), **le travail** (work), **le bateau** (boat), **le navet** (turnip), **le communisme** (communism), **le collège** (school), **le problème** (problem), **le vêtement** (garment)

- Words with the following endings are usually feminine: -ance, -anse, -ion, -ine, -tte, -ure.
  **la tendance** (tendency), **la danse** (dance), **la nation** (nation), **la cuisine** (kitchen, cooking), **la carotte** (carrot), **la nourriture** (food)

The **plural** of nouns is usually formed by adding **-s** as in English:

> table → **tables** (tables), chanson → **chansons** (songs)
> vélo → **vélos** (bikes), train → **trains** (trains)

Note that the final **-s** is not pronounced.

There are a number of exceptions:

- For nouns ending in **-au**, **-eau**, **-eu**, add **-x** to form the plural:
  **des tuyaux** (pipes), **des bateaux** (boats), **des neveux** (nephews)

- Some nouns ending in **-ou** also form the plural with **-x**:
  **les genoux** (knees), **des choux** (cabbages), **des bijoux** (jewels)

- For nouns ending in **-al**, the plural is usually formed by substituting **-aux** for **-al**:
  **des journaux** (newspapers), **des chevaux** (horses)

- Nouns ending in **-s**, **-z**, **-x** do not change in the plural:
  **des radis** (radishes), **les nez** (noses), **les prix** (prices)

**Adjectives** in French agree with nouns in number and gender and usually go *after* the noun:

> **un vin blanc** (a white wine), **deux vins blancs** (two white wines)
> **une rue étroite** (a narrow street), **des rues étroites** (narrow streets)

However, a few very common adjectives always go *before* the noun. These are:

> **bon/bonne** (good) – **un bon repas** (a good meal)
> **beau/belle** (beautiful, lovely) – **une belle maison** (a lovely house)
> **mauvais** (bad) – **du mauvais temps** (bad weather)
> **grand** (big, tall) – **un grand bâtiment** (a tall building)
> **gros/grosse** (big, large) – **une grosse somme** (a large sum)
> **petit** (small, little) – **un petit garçon** (a little boy)

The **plural** of adjectives is formed in the same way as for nouns. The **feminine** of adjectives is usually formed by adding **-e**:

> froid → **froide** (cold), chaud → **chaude** (hot)

There are exceptions which need to be learned individually but here are some patterns:

| masc. ending | feminine | example |
|---|---|---|
| in **-c** | **-che** | blanc → **blanche** |
| in **-x** | **-se** | heureux → **heureuse** |
| in **-er** | **-ère** | léger → **légère** |

| in -eau | -elle | beau → belle |
| in -ou | -olle | fou → folle |

Most **adverbs** are formed by adding **-ment** to the feminine form of the adjective:

**lent** (slow) → **lentement** (slowly)

Common adverbs not formed in this way are **bien** (well) and **mal** (badly).

**Possessive adjectives** (*my, your, his* etc) in French agree in number and gender with the noun that follows, unlike in English where they agree with the "possessor". For example:

he's lost *his* diary **il a perdu son agenda** (agenda is masculine)
she's lost *her* diary **elle a perdu son agenda** (agenda is masculine)
he's lost *his* keys **il a perdu ses clés** (clés is plural)
she's lost *her* keys **elle a perdu ses clés** (clés is plural)

Shown below are the masculine, feminine and plural forms for each:

| my | **mon, ma, mes** |
| your[1] | **ton, ta, tes** |
| his/her/its | **son, sa, ses** |
| our | **notre, notre, nos** |
| your[2] | **votre, votre, vos** |
| their | **leur, leur, leurs** |

[1] Informal, talking to one person.
[2] Talking to more than one person or to one person you do not know well.

The **subject pronouns** (*I, you, we* etc) are as follows:

| **je** (I) | **nous** (we) |
| **tu** (you[1]) | **vous** (you[2]) |
| **il** (he, it[3]), **elle** (she, it[3]) | **ils, elles** (they[3]) |

[1] Informal, talking to one person.
[2] Talking to more than one person or to one person you do not know well.
[3] Depending on the gender in French of who or what is being referred to.

French distinguishes between direct object pronouns (I like *them*) and indirect object pronouns (I gave *them* the address = I gave the address *to them*).
The **direct object pronouns** (*me, you* etc) are as follows:

| **me** (me) | **nous** (us) |
| **te** (you[1]) | **vous** (you[2]) |
| **le** (him, it[3]), **la** (her, it[3]) | **les** (them) |

[1] Informal talking to one person.

[2] Talking to more than one person or to one person you do not know well.

[3] Depending on the gender in French of what is being referred to.

Note that **me**, **te**, **le/la** become **m'**, **t'**, **l'** before a word beginning with a vowel.

> **il m'a vu** he saw me
>
> **je t'appellerai ce soir** I'll ring you tonight

The **indirect object pronouns** (*(to) me, (to) you* etc) are as follows:

| | |
|---|---|
| **me** (me) | **nous** (us) |
| **te** (you[1]) | **vous** (you[2]) |
| **lui** (him, her, it) | **leur** (them) |

[1] Informal, talking to one person.

[2] Talking to more than one person or to one person you do not know well.

> **elle lui a envoyé une carte** she sent him/her a card
>
> **je leur ai donné mon adresse** I gave them my address

**Possessive pronouns** are the words we use to say who something belongs to: this is *mine* and that's *yours*. French adds the information on the gender and number of what it is that belongs to the person.

> **le mien/la mienne/les miens/les miennes** (mine)
>
> **le tien/la tienne/les tiens/les tiennes** (yours[1])
>
> **le sien/la sienne/les siens/les siennes** (his, hers, its[3])
>
> **le/la nôtre/les nôtres** (ours)
>
> **le/la vôtre/les vôtres** (yours[2])
>
> **le/la leur/les leurs** (theirs)

[1] Informal talking to one person.

[2] Talking to more than one person or to one person you do not know well.

[3] Depending on the gender in French of who or what is being referred to.

Note that people will often prefer to say: **c'est à moi/à toi/à eux** (it's mine/yours/theirs) to indicate possession. These are called **disjunctive pronouns**. They are used after prepositions and in statements like **c'est moi !** (it's me!). The disjunctive pronouns are:

| | |
|---|---|
| **moi** (me, I) | **nous** (we, us) |
| **toi** (you) | **vous** (you) |
| **lui** (him, he, it), **elle** (her, she, it) | **eux, elles** (them, they) |

> **c'est pour toi** it's for you
>
> **les verres sont à eux** the glasses are theirs
>
> **moi, je crois que …** I think that …

**Reflexive pronouns** are used when the subject and the object of the verb are identical: I saw *myself* in the mirror. In French these are:

| | |
|---|---|
| **me** (myself) | **nous** (ourselves) |
| **te** (yourself[1]) | **vous** (yourselves[2]) |
| **se** (himself, herself, itself) | **se** (themselves) |

[1] Informal, talking to one person.
[2] Talking to more than one person or to one person you do not know well.
Note that **te** and **se** become **t'** and **s'** before a word beginning with a vowel.

il **s'**est blessé he's hurt *himself*

In French some verbs that carry an idea of doing something to oneself are **reflexive verbs**, so are used with a reflexive pronoun. These are shown in the dictionary section. Examples are:

je me réveille I wake up
je me lève I get up

French **verbs** are divided into three groups (conjugations), ending in -**er**, -**ir** and -**re**.
Here is the **present tense** of three regular verbs, one from each conjugation. A hyphen has been inserted only so that you can see the endings more clearly:

| **parler** | **finir** | **attendre** |
|---|---|---|
| je parl-**e** | je fin-**is** | j'attend-**s** |
| tu parl-**es** | tu fin-**is** | tu attend-**s** |
| il/elle parl-**e** | il/elle fin-**it** | il/elle attend |
| nous parl-**ons** | nous fin-**issons** | nous attend-**ons** |
| vous parl-**ez** | vous fin-**issez** | vous attend-**ez** |
| ils/elles parl-**ent** | ils/elles fin-**issent** | ils/elles attend-**ent** |

vous parlez très bien français you speak very good French
ils finissent leur repas they're finishing their meal
je t'attends dehors I'll wait for you outside

There are also a number of irregular verbs which have to be learnt. Here are some common irregular verbs in the present tense:

| **être**[1] (to be) | **avoir**[1] (to have) | **aller** (to go) |
|---|---|---|
| je suis | j'ai | je vais |
| tu es | tu as | tu vas |
| il/elle est | il/elle a | il/elle va |
| nous sommes | nous avons | nous allons |

| vous êtes | vous avez | vous allez |
| ils/elles sont | ils/elles ont | ils/elles vont |

| **faire** (to do) | **venir** (to come) | **dire** (to say) |
|---|---|---|
| je fais | je viens | je dis |
| tu fais | tu viens | tu dis |
| il/elle fait | il/elle vient | il/elle dit |
| nous faisons | nous venons | nous disons |
| vous faites | vous venez | vous dites |
| ils/elles font | ils/elles viennent | ils/elles disent |

| **devoir** (to have to) | **pouvoir** (to come) | **vouloir** (to want) |
|---|---|---|
| je dois | je peux | je veux |
| tu dois | tu peux | tu veux |
| il/elle doit | il/elle peut | il/elle veut |
| nous devons | nous pouvons | nous voulons |
| vous devez | vous pouvez | vous voulez |
| ils/elles doivent | ils/elles peuvent | ils/elles veulent |

| **mettre** (to put) | **voir** (to see) | **savoir** (to know) |
|---|---|---|
| je mets | je vois | je sais |
| tu mets | tu vois | tu sais |
| il/elle met | il/elle voit | il/elle sait |
| nous mettons | nous voyons | nous savons |
| vous mettez | vous voyez | vous savez |
| ils/elles mettent | ils/elles voient | ils/elles savent |

[1] **Être** and **avoir** are also used as *auxiliary verbs* when forming the **present perfect** tense.

**Avoir** is used for most verbs:

   j'**ai** acheté un pantalon I've bought some trousers

   **as**-tu vu ce film ? have you seen this film?

**Être** is used to form the present perfect tense of verbs of motion and change of state:

   elle **est** allé<u>e</u>* au cinéma she's gone to the cinema

   ils **sont** venu<u>s</u>* ici l'année dernière they came here last year

*Note that when a verb forms its present perfect with **être**, the past participle agrees in gender and number with the subject of the verb.

The **imperfect** tense is used to express a continuous action in the past (eg I *was talking* to him). Here is how to form the imperfect tense for regular verbs:

| parler | finir | attendre |
|---|---|---|
| je parl-**ais** | je fin-**issais** | j'attend-**ais** |
| tu parl-**ais** | tu fin-**issais** | tu attend-**ais** |
| il/elle parl-**ait** | il/elle fin-**issait** | il/elle attend-**ait** |
| nous parl-**ions** | nous fin-**issions** | nous attend-**ions** |
| vous parl-**iez** | vous fin-**issiez** | vous attend-**iez** |
| ils/elles parl-**aient** | ils/elles fin-**issaient** | ils/elles attend-**aient** |

The imperfect of **être** is: j'étais, tu étais, il/elle était, nous étions, vous étiez, ils/elles étaient.

The imperfect of **avoir** is: j'avais, tu avais, il/elle avait, nous avions, vous aviez, ils/elles avaient.

The **future** tense is usually formed by adding the following endings to the infinitive:

-**ai**, -**as**, -**a**, -**ons**, -**ez**, -**ont**

Example with **parler**: je parlerai, tu parleras, il/elle parlera, nous parlerons, vous parlerez, ils/elles parleront.

> **je lui parlerai demain** I'll talk to him/her tomorrow
> **le match finira à 17h** the match will finish at 5pm

# HOLIDAYS AND FESTIVALS

## NATIONAL BANK HOLIDAYS

In France, bank holidays are known as **jours fériés**. Administrative offices, banks, offices and most shops are closed.

| | |
|---|---|
| 1 January | **le jour de l'an**, also known as **le nouvel an** (New Year's Day) |
| March/April | **lundi de Pâques** (Easter Monday) |
| 1 May | **le premier mai**, **fête du travail** (Labour Day) |
| 8 May | **le 8 mai** (VE Day, celebrating the end of the German occupation of France in the Second World War) |
| May | **le jeudi de l'Ascension** (Ascension) |
| 14 July | **le 14 juillet** (French National Day, celebrating the storming of the Bastille in 1789) |
| 15 August | **l'Assomption** (Assumption) |
| 1 November | **la Toussaint** (All Saints' Day) |
| 11 November | **le 11 novembre**, also known as **l'Armistice** (Armistice Day, celebrating the end of the First World War) |
| 25 December | **Noël** (Christmas Day) |

## FESTIVALS

The French love festivals. Every village holds its own, mainly during the summer months. There are also numerous cultural festivals held throughout the year.

| | |
|---|---|
| January | Some town and villages still celebrate **carnival** but the custom is no longer widespread. A notable exception is the northern city of Dunkirk where celebrations and parades are held from 24 January until 13 March. |
| February | Another internationally known carnival is held in Nice, on the Mediterranean coast. Some of the traditions include the Battle of the Flowers parade, the **carnastring** (a dip in the Baie des Anges on the first Sunday of the festival) and the **carnacourse**, a race for waiters in which they can show off their tray-carrying skills. And of course there are the traditional parades and fireworks. |

| May | The **Festival international du film de Cannes** is without doubt the most important cinematic event in the world. Every year a whole host of stars descend on the Mediterranean resort. The winning film is awarded the prestigious **palme d'or** (golden palm) award. |

June
A major national event is the **Festival de la musique** which is held on 21 June, the first day of summer and is celebrated in town and villages all over the country. Every type of music has its place, from classical to rock, reggae and folk. Events are publicized well in advance and range from gala concerts in prestigious venues to an endless variety of street music.

On **la Saint-Jean** (Midsummer's Day: 24 June) it is the custom in many areas to light bonfires. Traditionally people jump over these in order to prevent the winter's cold from returning.

July
Another major cultural event takes place every year in Avignon, the seat of the Pope in the 14th century and situated on the banks of the Rhone. The **Festival d'Avignon** features music, dance and open-air theatre. The official programme is accompanied by the "**off**" festival, seen as a springboard for young talent.

A major French sporting event is the **Tour de France**. For the three weeks of the race the whole country is gripped, with passions running high. Whenever the cyclists pass through a town or village, everything stops and a real party atmosphere breaks out.

14 July
The French national day is a celebration of the storming of the Bastille prison (**la prise de la Bastille**) in 1789, during the French Revolution. It is the most important festival of the year, and even the tiniest villages put on a **bal** (dance) and firework displays.

November
**La fête du beaujolais** is celebrated each year on 18 November, the date on which the year's new vintage, **le beaujolais nouveau**, comes onto the market. The beaujolais wine-growing region lies just to the north of Lyons. Cafés and restaurants all over the country put on festive events at which the new wine can be sampled and a big celebration is held in the region's capital, Villefranche-sur-Saône.

# USEFUL ADDRESSES

## IN FRANCE

### British Embassy
35, rue du Faubourg Saint-Honoré 70008 Paris
Tel: 01 44 51 31 00

There are British Consulates in the other four big cities in France. If you have a problem, you should contact the nearest one. The telephone numbers are:

Bordeaux: 05 57 22 21 10
Lyon: 04 72 77 81 70

Lille: 03 20 12 82 72
Marseille: 04 91 15 72 10

### Irish Embassy
4, rue Rude 75016 Paris
Tel: 01 44 17 67 00

### Tourist Information – Paris
127, avenue des Champs-Élysées 75008 Paris
Tel: 01 49 52 53 54

## IN THE UK

### French Embassy – London
58, Knightsbridge London SW1X 7JT
Tel: 0207 073 1000

### French Tourist Office – London
178, Piccadilly London W1J 9AL
Tel: 0207 499 6911

# CONVERSION TABLES

Note that when writing numbers, French uses a comma where English uses a full stop. For example 2.5 would be written 2,5 in French and spoken as *deux virgule cinq*.

## Measurements

Only the metric system is used in France.

**Length**
1 cm ≈ 0.4 inches
30 cm ≈ 1 foot

**Distance**
1 metre ≈ 1 yard
1 km ≈ 0.6 miles

To convert kilometres into miles, divide by 8 and then multiply by 5.

| kilometres | 1 | 2 | 5 | 10 | 20 | 100 |
|---|---|---|---|---|---|---|
| miles | 0.6 | 1.25 | 3.1 | 6.25 | 12.50 | 62.5 |

To convert miles into kilometres, divide by 5 and then multiply by 8.

| miles | 1 | 2 | 5 | 10 | 20 | 100 |
|---|---|---|---|---|---|---|
| kilometres | 1.6 | 3.2 | 8 | 16 | 32 | 160 |

**Weight**
25g ≈ 1 oz     1 kg ≈ 2 lb     6 kg ≈ 1 stone

To convert kilos into pounds, divide by 5 and then multiply by 11.
To convert pounds into kilos, multiply by 5 and then divide by 11.

| kilos | 1 | 2 | 10 | 20 | 60 | 80 |
|---|---|---|---|---|---|---|
| pounds | 2.2 | 4.4 | 22 | 44 | 132 | 176 |

**Liquid**
1 litre ≈ 2 pints
4.5 litres ≈ 1 gallon

**Temperature**

To convert temperatures in Celsius into Fahrenheit, divide by 5, multiply by 9 and then add 32.
To convert temperatures in Fahrenheit into Celsius, subtract 32, multiply by 5 and then divide by 9.

| **Celsius** (°C) | 0 | 4 | 10 | 15 | 20 | 30 | 38 |
|---|---|---|---|---|---|---|---|
| **Fahrenheit** (°F) | 32 | 40 | 50 | 59 | 68 | 86 | 100 |

## Clothes sizes

Sometimes you will find sizes given using the English-language abbreviations **XS**, **S**, **M**, **L** and **XL** and often, as in the UK, sizes from 1 to 4. Otherwise, see below:

• **Women's clothes**

| Europe | 36 | 38 | 40 | 42 | 44 | etc |
|---|---|---|---|---|---|---|
| UK | 8 | 10 | 12 | 14 | 16 | |

• **Bras** (cup sizes are the same)

| Europe | 70 | 75 | 80 | 85 | 90 | etc |
|---|---|---|---|---|---|---|
| UK | 32 | 34 | 36 | 38 | 40 | |

• **Men's shirts** (collar size)

| Europe | 36 | 38 | 41 | 43 | etc |
|---|---|---|---|---|---|
| UK | 14 | 15 | 16 | 17 | |

• **Men's clothes**

| Europe | 40 | 42 | 44 | 46 | 48 | 50 etc |
|---|---|---|---|---|---|---|
| UK | 30 | 32 | 34 | 36 | 38 | 40 |

**Shoe sizes**

• **Women's shoes**

| Europe | 37 | 38 | 39 | 40 | 42 | etc |
|---|---|---|---|---|---|---|
| UK | 4 | 5 | 6 | 7 | 8 | |

• **Men's shoes**

| Europe | 40 | 42 | 43 | 44 | 46 | etc |
|---|---|---|---|---|---|---|
| UK | 7 | 8 | 9 | 10 | 11 | |